The Zoë Life

Connect To Abundance Now!

Kristen Marie

Printed in the United States of America.

Unless otherwise indicated, all scriptures are taken from the New International Version (NIV) of the Bible.

ISBN 978-1-64085-954-8 (paperback)

ISBN 978-1-64085-955-5 (hardback)

ISBN 978-1-64085-956-2 (ebook)

Table of Contents

Jesus presented to them another parable,
saying,
"The kingdom of Heaven is like a
mustard seed,
which a man took and planted in his field.
It's the smallest of seeds;
yet when it's full grown,
it's greater than the other herbs.
It becomes *like a tree,*
so that the birds of the air come
and nest in its branches."

Matt. 13:32

Tree of Life Version

God's Dream

Who knows how long I had been lying there. I had lost track of time. Yet I wasn't bothered by it.

Instead, I wanted to bottle the moment and preserve it forever. There was no place I would rather be. The weather was perfect. The sun was shining bright, playfully peeking its face out from behind the billows of white clouds.

I lazily rested on my soft blanket within the shade of a gorgeous oak tree. My long, curly brown hair was pulled from behind my neck, wildly fanned out above my head. Occasionally, the light gentle breeze would catch my hair and softly caress my cheek. I liked when this happened. There was a faint scent of blooming flowers floating through the air. I could hear the singsong conversation between two birds, somewhere in the top of the tree. It seemed like time was standing still.

I had recently given my heart to Jesus and was beginning to read the Bible on a regular basis. As I was daydreaming, I found myself being drawn back to a verse that had snagged my heart a few weeks earlier when I was curled up on my bed in my college dorm room. I was casually reading, when suddenly, it popped off the page. It was John 10:10 where Jesus says: "I have come that they may have life and have it to the full!"

This revelation made my heart come alive! It gave me hope! Almost immediately, I began researching what Jesus meant by, "have life to the full." I quickly learned Greek was the original language in which this passage was written. And the Greek word for "life" is "*zoë*," translated "God's quality of life or life in its fullest sense"!

Jesus came to bring abundant life?!

My life was busy, but I wouldn't call it abundant.

I suddenly felt permission to dream about Jesus' plan for my future. *What does God mean by the "abundant life"? Do Christian millionaires encounter it? Did Mother Teresa experience the abundant life? Did she connect with what Jesus came to bring?*

From my perspective, many Christians *I knew* wouldn't say they were living the zoë, abundant life. And this disconnect bothered me. So I pondered these things, and decided I would do further research to discover what was missing. I found there is so much more to Christian living than I had imagined. It's what happens *below* the surface that makes our lives healthy or sickly. It's what goes on behind closed doors and in the crevices of our minds that determine our positive outcomes. I learned God's preset patterns would bring us great joy and abundance, if only we will follow them.

Throughout these pages, I will use an oak tree as a metaphor to share my story of connecting to John 10:10. My desire is to help you shave off decades of needless struggle in your own journey and reveal how to connect with the zoë, abundant life.

The Abundant Zoë Full Life

I wasn't sure what the abundant life looked like. So I asked God, "Would You show me what it means to experience Your kind of life *in the fullest sense*? Would You help me to understand what abundance is *to You*?"

Instantly, He brought to mind the moment when I was lying on the ground beneath the oak tree. I remembered it well: As I was enjoying the peaceful breeze, I had been thinking about my current navigation through life, which was the use of a management tool that I had been introduced to eighteen months prior. It is called the Wheel of Life. It was designed to help people visually examine their life, assess where they are currently, and identify what changes they need to make in order to function more effectively. As I was pondering this, I realized it had been an incredibly helpful tool, but I realized God was about to show me a new way to bring order and peace to my life. But first, let's look at the wheel:

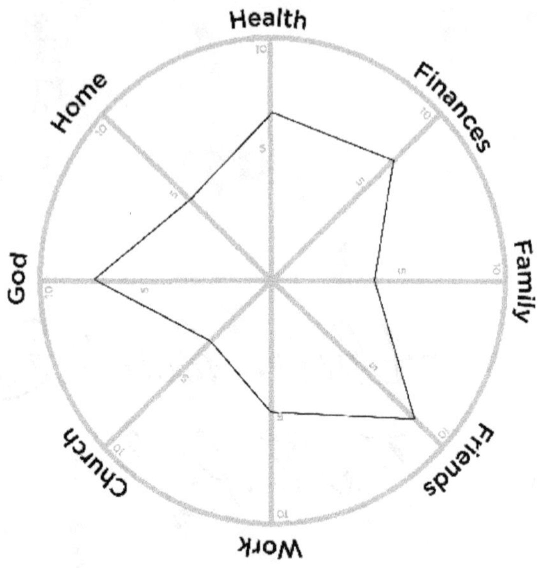

[Figure A—The Wheel of Life]

It is termed the Wheel of Life because it looks like a wheel. Each spoke represents a different aspect of life: spiritual, physical, professional, relational, and financial. (Some Wheels are more detailed than others.) The goal is to evaluate the spokes periodically to keep your life fully *balanced*, so that the *wheel* will roll smoothly. For some, the objective is for every spoke to maintain a ten out of ten in every category of one's life.

But according to this diagram, it seemed my life wasn't "rolling well." My spokes were out of balance, as they were at different levels of success. And the reason: God was becoming increasingly larger in my heart, mind, and emotions. Clearly, He had greater significance and value than the other parts. According to this model, my wheel would always be out of balance; due to the amount of time I spent seeking God. I believe my relationship with Him should ever-outweigh the other categories of my life. It is the expanding foundation by which those areas flourish. So I set out to create another life-management tool that reflected my ever-growing passion for Jesus, and doing this produced a well-balanced life for me!

Now, instead of seeing each aspect of my life as a "spoke" in a wheel, I imagined each facet looking like the cross section of a tree with concentric rings surrounding the inner core. Like a tree, the growth of each outer ring is directly connected to and affected by the health and fruitfulness of the ring before it.

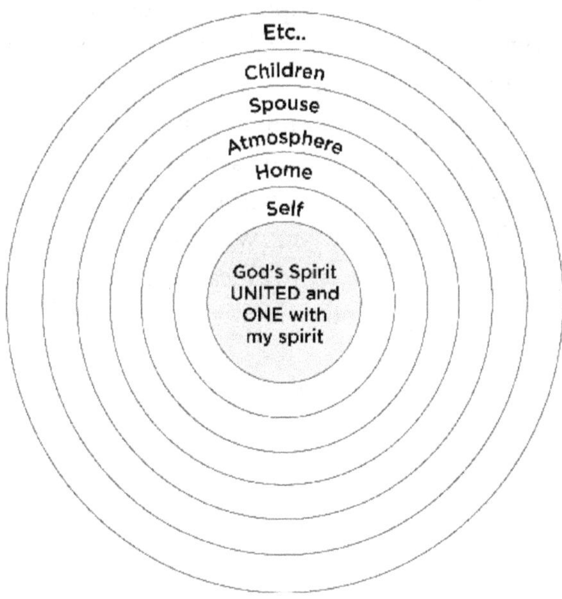

[Figure B—The Zoë Life]
zoë = *the God-designed life*

How do rings form?

In order to fully understand this metaphor, we must grasp the importance of how trees begin. A tree starts with a seed; it sprouts roots, and then becomes a seedling. Soon, the seedling forms a core, inner ring. Then, once this inner ring is established, another ring forms and then another, until it becomes a sapling. As this process continues over time, the external product (the life others see) will be like what Isaiah 61:3 calls "an oak tree of righteousness, planted by God, for the display of His splendor, glory, and goodness."

Looking back, I can see when I began actively using The Zoë Life diagram, a shift occurred in my story. I started to see and understand that every aspect of my life was indeed affected by my innermost being. So now, my energy was spent making sure the life of God was flowing from me, by applying His Word, and by spending time in His Presence. For over two decades, this visual tool has governed my life, by connecting me to the zoë, the abundance that Jesus spoke of in John 10:10. My new graphic would also help others on their path of life. My hope is the same for you!

I believe a transformation will occur as you discover the fullness of God's desire for you. Within each chapter, we will discuss how to maximize fruitfulness in your inner rings, so that your life displays God's glory, goodness, and splendor!

Now is the time . . .

Your Inner Ring Begins as a Seed

I remember being in kindergarten, on a weekend that I was staying with my dad.

I asked him, "Do you mind if I walk to that church a few blocks away?"

He didn't mind at all.

I loved going! I couldn't wait to hear the stories about God!

Really? Living three days in a fish's belly! I was so captivated.

Now, on the weekends, when I visited my mom, I didn't attend church because there wasn't one within walking distance. But a few years later, my grade-school friend occasionally invited me to attend with her family. I loved it and felt right at home.

When I was eleven years old, I moved in with my dad. He was newly married and had just relocated to the outskirts of a small town. It had a population of around 9,000 people. A large field separated us from our next-door neighbors, who were an elderly couple. I noticed that every Sunday morning, their car would leave before 10:00 a.m. and arrive back at home near noon. I assumed they were going to church.

So one day, I walked across the big field to their house. They probably thought "their little neighbor" was selling something, because our families didn't talk very often to each other.

I knocked on the door, and a gentleman in his seventies answered.

I said quickly, "Hi. My name is Kristen. I'm one of the kids that live next door. There are five boys and four girls, if we are all home at the same time. How are you?"

With a pleasant, welcoming smile, he said, "I'm fine. How can I help you?"

I responded, "Well, I noticed that every Sunday your car leaves in the mornings. I'm wondering if you are going to church?"

(Clearly, I didn't understand different denominations. I was simply interested in responding to the gnawing in my heart.)

"Well, yes, we do." He seemed pleased.

I said, "That's wonderful! How would you feel if I went to church with you on Sunday mornings?"

His wife was now standing beside him, also smiling with kind eyes. She tenderly said, "We would love for you to join us."

So that became the routine for most Sunday mornings. I was excited and eager, waiting for their station wagon to arrive in my driveway. Most of the time I sat in the backseat, the second row, but occasionally, I felt adventurous and asked if I could sit in the very back, where I faced the cars driving behind us. That was such an interesting feeling and perspective.

The Sunday school class was comprised of several grade levels grouped together. The other kids looked familiar to me. However, since I was one of the "new kids" in town, as well as in school, I didn't know their names. I recognized immediately they had been going to church for a long time—they knew all the answers to the questions the teacher asked.

After Sunday school, while sitting in "big church", I could see the other kids pointing and talking about me. For some reason I felt embarrassed, even though I didn't know what they were saying. I imagined they were discussing that the couple I was sitting with wasn't my family. As I reflect on that moment, I am still unsure why I felt uncomfortable seeing them whispering about me. Perhaps, I just wanted to feel accepted and invited to sit with their group.

Somewhere along the way, my season shifted. I started playing competitive soccer about an hour away. The games were on both Saturday and Sunday, so we were gone every weekend. I missed learning about God and hearing more about that guy named Jesus.

HIGH SCHOOL AND COLLEGE DAYS

When I was in high school, a small church would host "Fifth Quarter," a post football game get-together. I remember attending a few of them, even though I didn't attend the church. There was food to eat, ping-pong and pool to play, and people to catch up with. Each time a different person spoke for about fifteen minutes and ended their talk with, "If you died tonight and don't know if you will go to Heaven, then I want you to stand up and walk to the front and say, 'Yes!' to Jesus."

With much sincerity and my heart pounding out of my chest, I stood up and walked to the front ... *every time!* Then, during Christmas break my freshman year in college, I attended a four-night conference with a campus ministry. On the last night, they gave a similar invitation. Once again, the speaker was sharing about how simple and easy it was to "be saved." He said, "If you simply confess with your mouth that Jesus is Lord and believe in your heart that God raised Him from the dead, you will be saved."

I had confessed before. And I had believed before.

It wasn't more heartfelt this time, as I was just as sincere *all* the other times.

Yet this time it was *different.*

This time, it wasn't just about spending eternity in Heaven. This time, I didn't just feel like a "good person making the best decisions I could". This time, I felt unclean. I felt my filth. This time, I felt my need for help outside of what I could do for myself. This time, there was a heavy awareness of my sins and my independent spirit that I didn't experience or notice before. It was a brokenness, a cry and a desperation from my heart. This time, I wanted to *know* Jesus and have a daily dialogue with Him. I no longer wanted to feel alone or navigate through life on my own.

My heart was convinced that Jesus was the only answer to feeling clean and at peace. I wanted that. I wanted Him! I longed to feel pure and full of rest—for the lust of this world to go away. I needed His forgiveness for my sins. I realized, on my own I couldn't do anything to become clean and pure. I knew I needed help. Jesus was the only answer to real change.

So this time, when I said "Yes!" to Jesus, it was about surrendering. This time, when I said, "Yes, Jesus!" it was about *truly letting go*. I hadn't surrendered myself fully to Him and His care before. Finally, a death; a death to self. And *this death* was the beginning of a lifelong change in me.

"Unless a grain of wheat falls to the earth and dies,
it remains alone.
But if it dies, it produces many seeds and much fruit."
John 12:24

DYING SEEDS PRODUCE LIFE

Now, that I had chosen to die to self and to the sin in which all people are born, my transformation would be similar to that of a seed. Because it's not just about dying, but about what the death produces. So let's discuss this amazing process! When a seed is planted, it must go through a physical death. This dying process is actually a metamorphosis because it ceases to be "what it once was" and becomes "something new altogether"—like the inner ring of a tree.

For the inner ring of a tree to form, the coat of the seed breaks open so roots can emerge. These roots must undergo vivacious imbibition (which means to drink) to stimulate more root growth. As the seed begins to enlarge, taking in more water and oxygen, additional roots are produced. Eventually, a seedling and then a sapling, which is a very tiny tree, is formed.

When I discovered what happens in the dying of an oak tree *seed*, to eventually become an oak *tree*, I could see a parallel to the first few stages of my spiritual metamorphosis. First, my heart had to break open. Then I had to choose to surrender and let go of being in charge of my own life.

Once I said "Yes!" to Jesus *fully*, I experienced an awakening...my inner core (my spirit) was alive! I was a new creation, like a seed changing into a seedling, and then into a sapling. My "tree growth" process had begun. As I chose to intertwine my spirit with God's, the two became united as one, and I was inseparable with Him.

And just as a physical seed undergoes vivacious drinking for growth, I also experienced this need in my spiritual journey. I don't recall in times past having a desire to read the Bible, or spend time seeking Jesus. However, since my "Yes!" was different this time, I experienced a vibrant hunger and thirst that only more of Jesus could satisfy. As I chose to lean in to this hunger by feeding my spirit, roots quickly sprouted in my life.

> [NOTE: *As I reflect on my spiritual journey, I am so thankful for God's faithful pursuit of me. He continued to beckon me to Himself, again and again, until I experienced a true, total surrender. If you can't recall truly saying "Yes!" to Jesus*

and surrendering to Him, so that your seed experiences the death needed to sprout roots in God's abundant love, simply tell Him today. In your own words, tell Him that you want Him, that you want to give up your ways for Him and His ways. Choose to let Him bear the penalty for your sins, and exchange your old life for His Zoë life.]

Now is the time . . .

The Sapling

The lights were shining directly in my eyes. I couldn't see anyone in the audience. But I assumed there were at least two thousand people watching me. That was usually the size of the crowd for these special evenings.

Of course, I wished someone from my family was able to attend. Moments like this one are rare.

It was my turn next. For some reason, I felt nervous. Or perhaps, those were just butterflies in my belly. I continued to take steps forward, moving slowly lest I disrupt this consecrated moment.

I shivered.

I placed my right foot gently in the water. It was surprisingly warmer than I had expected.

Stepping deeper, I lowered myself into the water. Its warmth helped my body, thoughts and emotions to relax. It felt nice.

I smiled at the gentleman who was waiting on me. His countenance was shining, and although he didn't know me, he seemed so proud of me. I felt thankful for him.

He gently placed his hand on my upper back. Since we didn't know each other well, he asked me to make my confession of faith,

"Kristen, do you believe that Jesus Christ is the Son of God?"

"I do," I replied.

And with great delight and pride, he said, "I baptize you in the name of the Father, the Son, and the Holy Spirit."

Then I held my nose as he slowly leaned my body backwards until I was completely submerged (buried) by the water. As he helped lift me up, I could hear the audience cheering and clapping for me. The white gown I was wearing was symbolic of what had happened to me—clean, spotless, and pure! A smile beamed across my face, reflecting the joy in my heart.

Months before this special evening I was attending several different churches and participated in a variety of Bible studies. *When one of the churches announced for baptism, and to publically share outwardly with the world about any recent inward renewals, I had excitedly signed up!*

Just like when a person rises up from a water baptism, unveiling "new life," a tree that sprouts up from the ground reveals its new creation. The death of the seed has occurred, and the transformation is in process. Your life no longer looks like a seed, or even a seedling. Instead it looks more like a sapling—a young tree sprouting above the surface. Your life is intertwined and deeply connected with God's love, invitation and acceptance. The inner conversion is no longer hidden from others. He designed your "new look" for all to see. And the next steps of your life are spent building upon this new foundation.

INCREASING THE CORE, INNER RING

Years ago, I remember coming across a chart illustrating the triune aspect of a person's being. It was a big circle, and inside was three smaller circles, each equal in size. The first one was labeled "spirit," the second, "soul" and the third, "body."

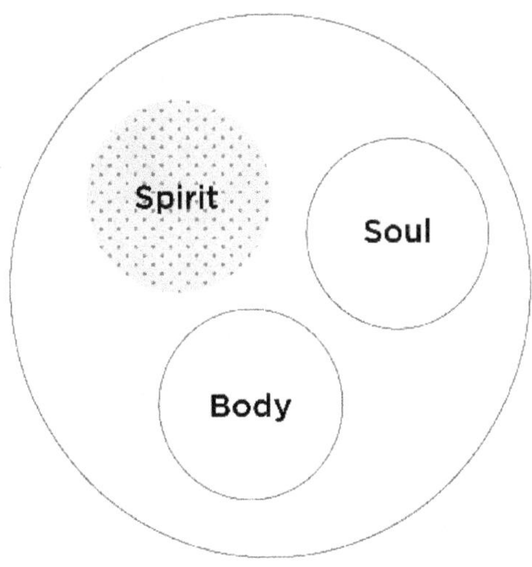

[Figure C—Triune aspects of a person's being (version 1)]

When I looked at the diagram, I couldn't connect with it. The diagram looked so perfect and proportional. *Three equal parts? When I said, "Yes!" to Jesus, I don't think my new creation was as "put together" as the diagram showed.* When I decided to follow Him, it seemed my spirit felt like an itty-bitty circle—perhaps the size of a mustard seed, while the majority of myself was still full of my old habits, thoughts, desires, and feelings.

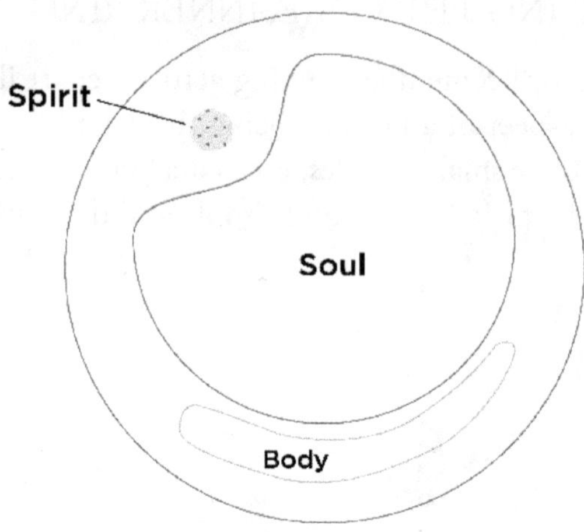

[Figure D—Triune aspects of a person's being (version 2)]

The following illustration is probably a better representation of what my "new self" looked like. Here, a larger soul and body surrounded the center of my being, where God's Spirit is located.

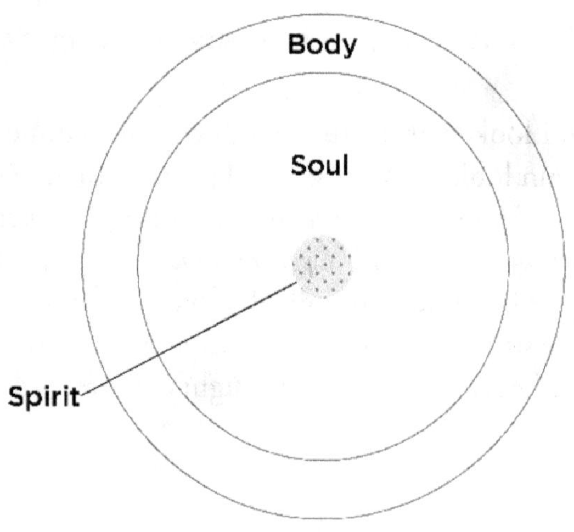

[Figure E—Triune aspects of a person's being (version 3)]

At this miniscule measure, I knew my little sapling wouldn't have the strength to survive life's storms. Something had to be done! I understood our life choices directly affected our spiritual journey. So that meant I was the one who would decide how large or influential God's Spirit would be in my life. I realized, even though my seed had died, and my surrender to Jesus was real, the habits of my old life were still engrained in the rhythms of my day. I needed to create new cycles that would cause my spirit to grow from an itty-bitty circle, to one that dominated my core. These new cycles, or right choices would allow my "tree" to be properly nourished, so it could grow from a sapling into an oak tree of righteousness. This is how God says it:

Deuteronomy 30:19: "Today, I call Heaven and Earth as witnesses against you, and I set before you life and death, blessings and curses. Now *choose life*, so that you and your children may live." (Emphasis mine)

Within time, I discovered the intentional *choose-life choices* did make my spirit grow larger in my inner core. It will be the same with you. As you feed your spirit, it will increase. It's *your choice.*

THE COMPARE AND CONTRAST DIAGRAMS

Below are two diagrams, which illustrate the contrast of those who choose to make right choices versus those who do not. Each shows the core of the born-again person united with God, Jesus and the Holy Spirit. Both illustrations reveal the fact, that because God's Spirit lives inside of us, "we have been given all things for life, godliness, glory and excellence" (2 Peter 1:3).

In the first illustration, the born-again believer has an itty-bitty core because he or she has not made the choose-life choices needed to feed, expand, and increase God's Spirit on the inside.

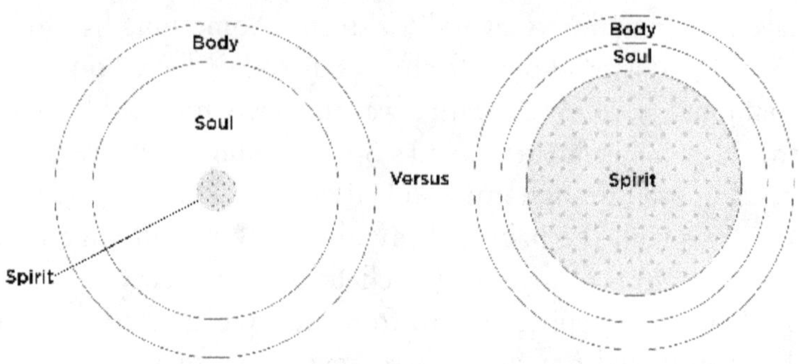

[Figure F—Comparison of diagrams showing triune aspects of a person's being]

The second illustration reveals the effects of a born-again person making many choose-life choices, so that God's Spirit is large and dominate inside of him or her -- full of His divine power, wisdom and strength.

Which illustration reflects the core of your sapling?

Will your sapling grow into a healthy, abundant, oak tree of righteousness?

It is for you to choose.

If your circle looks like the first illustration, don't be discouraged, as we will discuss solutions in further sections!

Now is the time . . .

Food for Your Core

As a certified personal trainer and exercise physiologist, I have trained many men and women to achieve their physical goals. To be successful, it is essential for each client to properly strengthen his or her core, as it is the most important muscle group in our body. The core is the system surrounding and supporting the spine and pelvis, while connecting the upper body and lower body together. Just as it is essential to care for our physical core, it is important for us to care for our spiritual, inner core by deliberately making choose-life choices. That is the purpose for this chapter: Listing some examples of *the food* your core needs so that God's Spirit can grow within you.

Remember: The goal and desire are for your core, or inner ring of the "tree" to be more substantial than your soul, or the mind, will, and emotions. Also keep in mind; the John 10:10 zoë abundance only occurs when God's Spirit increases in you. So the more you feed your core, the greater God's Spirit will be in your life. It is the same concept for everyone. Little by little, you integrate more choose-life choices into your days, and little by little, God's Spirit expands, until one day, you will operate in the Spirit's fullness. (There is no timeline for this. It is different for everyone. But definitely expect the best!)

RECEIVE FROM HIM

The first choose-life choice I recommend for feeding your core is learning the concept of *receiving from God.* There is no greater decision you can make than to *be still and receive Jesus' abundant, zoë love* for you. Doing this expresses your faith in God, and *faith* is what activates His supernatural power in your life.

Your spirit will soar when you simply choose to be still and be loved by Jesus. The key is stillness, silence, and solitude. It is an *active* lingering, while you engage your mind on His promises and supremacy until you feel His presence saturate every part of your being. This will expand your spiritual roots in the width, height, and depth of God's love for you. It will cast out fear, and absolutely, increase your fellowship with God.

So, commit to sit, be still, and actively wait upon God while meditating on His word and ways. Wait until His weighty Presence washes over you, until He saturates you with revelation of His Word and His will for your life. This is a choose-life choice.

This is no one way to hear and discern God's voice. There's no right or wrong way to do this, but I find that sitting, or lying in a quiet environment with my hands facing upward, helps my physical body prepare my spiritual body to receive.

Remaining in this position, can feel beautiful—we are to be undone by Him, receiving Him into our core, and allowing our body to feel His Spirit expand inside of us. This process may even feel like a warm, refining fire that is sizzling off the dross (the extra aspects of you) that get in the way of fully receiving Him.

COMMUNION (OR THE PASSOVER MEAL)

Another choose-life choice that I recommend is *taking Communion*. Taking Communion always involves physical "elements," such as grape juice and a cracker, which symbolize Jesus' precious blood and body. The focus of taking Communion is about Jesus, not the elements.

For me, it is easiest to take Communion when no one is present, so I can concentrate on His sacrifice. I want to thoroughly receive the cleansing and renewal offered by His broken body and His poured-out blood. Taking Communion corporately is also special, but I truly enjoy partaking in Him privately. I like it because I can go at my own pace. I prefer to let the Holy Spirit highlight anything and everything that needs to be acknowledged before God. Now, let's read this important conversation Jesus had with His disciples, right before He went to the cross:

> *"And He said to them, "I have eagerly desired to eat this Passover with you before I suffer."*
> *"And He took bread, gave thanks and broke it, and gave it to them, saying, 'This is my body given for you; do this in remembrance of me.' In the same way, after the supper He took the cup, saying, 'This cup is the new covenant in my blood, which is poured out for you'."*
> Luke 22:15, 19–20

Jesus called it Passover because the Jews had been keeping this tradition every year, using a lamb. The lamb would be the sacrifice to push away Israel's sins until the next year, but Jesus is called the Lamb of God because He was the *last* sacrifice. He made a way for the sins of the world to be eradicated forever.

Before I take Communion, I acknowledge all of this and put my faith fully in Jesus. I pause and utter my thanksgiving and praise to Jesus for His sacrifice. I close my eyes and picture Him standing about 8–12 inches right in front of me. Then, I slow down the process, and look intently into His smiling eyes and notice the beautiful lines in His face. Some days, Jesus takes one stride forward, to step completely into my being. And with much peace and pleasure, I receive His Presence. Other times, I initiate it by taking one step toward Him, causing myself to walk fully into Him.

Either way, the intimate union occurs. I can feel the oneness, and I relish it. I do not rush. I enjoy and feel the absolute delight of the moment. We are truly saturating each other. I am in Him, and He is in me. And it is from this oneness that I operate each moment of my day. My heart's desire is to choose life again and again, so that I remain tethered to this relationship — never stepping out of intimate fellowship with Him.

READING AND MEDITATING ON SCRIPTURE

A very transformative choose-life choice is *reading and meditating on the Bible*. Reading and meditating on God's very words will delight your spirit. Because the more you learn about Him, the greater your satisfaction! Even at times when God's Word seems dry or mundane, your spirit always rejoices. Your spirit is designed to feast on it day and night. The following scripture reveals how success in life comes:

> *"This book of the law shall not depart out of your mouth, but you shall meditate on it day and night, that you may observe and do according to all that is written in it. For then you shall make your way prosperous, and then you shall deal wisely and have good success."*
> Joshua 1:8

Learning about God and meditating on His ways found in the Bible will induce life-changing encounters with Him. When we experience His holiness during these encounters, we are inspired to "observe" and to "do" all He has written. Perceiving how incredibly majestic and holy He is will help you discover more about "the new you," since you are made in His image. So choose life by opening God's Word to feed on it daily. Study it. Ponder it. Become it.

In John 1:14 it says, "the Word became flesh." Let the scriptures come alive within you! The Word is essential for your core, inner ring to grow and expand inside you.

PRAYER

Prayer is another choose-life choice that will increase and grow your inner core. Through *prayer—dialoguing with God often*—we learn what is on His heart. He also learns what is on ours, and then sends breakthroughs our way. There are tremendous benefits in praying: Prayer keeps our spirit alert, warning us of danger. It also keeps us in sync with God, releasing blessings.

For me, prayer is simply what is says in Ephesians 6:18, "dialoguing with Him in the Spirit on all occasions with all kinds of prayers and requests; staying alert and persistent in my prayers for all God's people."

Asking of God is powerful. He has told us to "ask, seek and knock." So we know when we *ask* of Him anything according to His will, He hears us and will answer. He will not leave us in the dark. So be persistent in *seeking* His ways. Don't be afraid to *knock* on the door of His heart in any matter.

If you want to lean more into God through prayer, ask Him to "grow your passion." Ask Him to "increase your desire" for Him. For years, I would *ask*, "May I love You with all my heart, all my soul, all my mind, and all my strength?" I believe He continues to deepen my adoration of Him in answer to my request.

Additionally, I prefer praying in my prayer language. In John 7:38, Jesus says, "whoever believes in Me, rivers of living water will flow from their core, inner man," and that is exactly where I feel the Heavenly languages originate. Praying in my prayer language alerts my spirit man to be more receptive to what God's Spirit is saying. I can feel it burning inside. It eradicates the clutter from my thoughts and ideas and allows me to hear God more clearly.

SEEING AND HEARING

Another choose-life choice is *heightening your spirit's ability to see and hear*. Throughout the Bible, we learn about people who "have eyes to see and ears to hear." (Eph. 1:15–19) Most of the time, it was related to those who needed to have the right perspective, in order to receive the fullness of God. In Revelation 2:7, it emphasizes giving heed to what the Spirit says. So we must take His voice seriously. We must create a lifestyle of leaning into Him, to hear what *He* is saying and see how *He* is moving. When we do this, it is one of the most rewarding things on the face of the earth—to know God and connect with what is on His heart.

The ability to see and hear with your spirit does not need to be "imparted to you" by man. It is already inside of you by way of the Holy Spirit. This choose-life choice is about focusing and connecting with the Holy Spirit. He is a very real Person who baptizes us into what God is thinking and saying. The Holy Spirit shares God's intentions for us and shows us how to navigate through relationships and situations. So we must tune our spirit to know what He wants us to do, practically.

Part of this tuning is developing a rhythm of closing your eyes, to shut out the external environment. Then, as we wait and focus on connecting to the voice and thoughts of the Spirit of God, He will show us what is unseen. He will reveal the wisdom, discernment, knowledge, and understanding we need, which are all attributes of having eyes to see and ears to hear. *Continually* building your relationship with the Holy Spirit in this manner will help develop all your spiritual gifts. And in the process, you will find your spiritual voice has grown louder and stronger.

Of course, you may not hear God's voice every time you sit and wait for it. It may come "as you go." And sometimes, there are issues in your heart that hinder you from hearing and seeing. The most common reason is unforgiveness. But we learn how to forgive and press past any issue that holds us back. When we wrestle with God over anything, it builds intimacy with Him. It makes our bond stronger. And that is the purpose of our Christian walk!

RECORDING NIGHT DREAMS

It has been said, "If God can't talk to you during the day, He may sometimes use the night." So I keep a journal near my bed, or even my phone, for an audio recording. *Chronicling your nighttime dreams* is a great choose-life choice. Many patriarchs and kings in the Bible were warned or given instruction through dreams.

Job 33:15 says, "in a dream, a vision at night, when men and women are deep in sleep, fast asleep in their beds—God opens their ears and impresses them with warnings to turn them back from something bad they're planning, from some reckless choice, and keep them from an early grave, from the river of no return."

Now, once I have recorded my dreams, I use several trustworthy *Christian* dream interpretation books to help me understand any symbolism or typical meanings. Some of the standard topics are people, numbers, names, items, and colors. Although dreams offer very helpful information for present situations and circumstances, they can be like vanishing ink. Some of the details are difficult to remember unless they are recorded immediately—even in the middle of the night.

FASTING

Fasting is another choose-life choice that will greatly increase your spiritual capacity. It will also heighten you to the will of God in any given, or desperate situation. Just take Queen Esther, who led all of Israel to fast for three days from food and water, to save her people from death! Of course, fasting from anything, albeit, TV, social media, caffeine, sugar, bread, and other pleasures in your life is very beneficial. My preferred method is to abstain from eating food.

By choosing to miss a few scheduled meals for the day, or a period of days, you will find that you have to pull on God and cling to Him, no matter where you are or what you are doing. You will have a reliance and an awareness of Him and His Presence that is rare. Even when you are doing the dishes or laundry, transporting kids, running errands, or catching up with friends, you will be sensitive to His voice.

But the most powerful way of fasting is to go away in solitude to pray and commune with Jesus, while you are on the fast. Jesus told His disciples, who could not cast out a specific devil, that certain kinds will only come out through fasting and prayer. So remember, fasting *and* prayer make your spirit powerful!

Additionally, it is through fasting that you can relate to more Bible verses. For example, passages like Psalm 42:1, "As the deer pants for streams of water, so my soul pants for you, my God," and lyrics in worship songs such as, "nothing I desire compares to you" will most likely come alive. By choosing to fast frequently and consistently, you will develop the habit of leaning into, listening, and loving Him deeply, as well as enlarging your core.

Fasting from food is a beautiful way to reset your life from anything unhealthy, including bad habits, or strongholds. One time, I gained back my natural rhythm of going to bed on time and waking up early, through an extended water-only fast.

For those who are beginning a lifestyle of fasting and prayer, it is recommended to start like a runner who is training for a race. For example, they begin by walking, and over time, they increase their distance. Then, they start to jog. Runners usually enter a 5K before attempting a 10K or 15K. An extended, water-only fast can be compared to a "marathon."

Similarly, you want a gradual approach to abstaining from foods. At first, cut out "certain foods" for a period of time, like Daniel 1:12. Then perhaps commit to drinking only natural juices before fasting from all foods. There are some good books that can help anyone get started. Make sure and do a little research on what is best for you. And if you have any health issues, it's always best to ask your doctor before fasting of any kind.

WAKING EARLY AND IN THE MIDDLE OF THE NIGHT

Waking early or in the middle of the night is a mainstay for those who want to spend longer periods of time alone with the Lord. This choose-life choice is foundational, as Jesus Himself rose early to speak with His Father in Heaven. For me, it is easier to stay up late, than to wake up early. But over time, I have become more disciplined to go to bed early. Also, I have developed a routine of asking Jesus before going to sleep, "Will You wake me in the middle of the night to spend quality, uninterrupted time with You?" When He wakes me up, it feels like He is initiating a sweet rendezvous. I get excited and never regret the sleep I lost in order to spend time with Him.

Over the years, my daughters have occasionally seen me in the middle of the night, awake and alert so I can receive Jesus' love. They ended up joining me in these moments. Consequently, they have learned to love these encounters too. Often, they ask if I will wake them, so they won't miss a session with Him. I love how they are learning to value these special moments with Jesus!

MINISTERING TO THE LORD

Finally, one of my favorite choose-life choices is *ministering to the Lord.* Acts 13:2, reveals the phrase, "As they ministered to the Lord." This is simply worshiping, praising, and loving on Him—God, Jesus, and the Holy Spirit. It is flooding Him with all of you.

Ministering to the Lord is about thanksgiving and rejoicing. It is about adoring and welcoming Him with no strings attached. It is delighting in Him and blessing Him with honor. Whether you do this through humming, singing, dancing, or through picturing scenes with Him in your thoughts, revere Him with the meditations of your heart.

No matter the style, rhythm or process of connection, ministering to the Lord is about feeling the oneness between the two of you. It is a full-circle moment. It is about receiving Him and His love fully, and offering yourself and your love, fully. Ministering to Him is when you completely embrace your identity as belonging to *Him*!

GROWING IN EVERY SEASON

Over time, and by God's grace, it has become easier for me to feel strongly connected to God's Spirit, and to stay in communion with Him, even in the mundane, everyday activities. This has allowed me to produce growth in every season, as I have learned the rhythm of His ways—The Zoë Life.

The same can be true *for you.*

No matter where you are, you can start *now* . . . even in this very moment. As your core grows and matures, you will find yourself living and being guided by the Holy Spirit (Rom. 8:14). The mature oak tree of righteousness in you is waiting for you to *choose life* so that it can reveal itself and shine God's glory, goodness, and splendor.

Now is the time . . .

Your Healthy Trunk Living from the Inside Out

In the last chapter, I only listed a few choose-life choices that if applied, will lead to an overcoming life. There are many more in the Bible. As you look for opportunities to make these choices in your daily routine, they will become your foundational habits for life. Your spiritual connection with God will be intimate and strong, impenetrable by the enemy's devices. You will experience more and more victories, and less and less defeat because you will be living life from the *overflow* of what is happening inside of you, or your healthy trunk. Now, let's read a true story, modern-day parable!

THE SURFACE LEVEL CHRISTIAN AND A HOLLOW TREE

After several years of marriage, my husband and I decided to embark upon an adventure. We wanted to build a home. And I was excited! One of my natural gifts is beautifying spaces. I enjoy discussing floor plans, coordinating colors, and determining which aesthetics are best for designing. I love turning a house into a home!

One day, a half-acre lot caught our attention. I drove past it for months. It was in a lovely neighborhood. There were several ponds, walking trails, and thirty acres of urban forest. Also, there was a basketball court, a playground, a neighborhood pool, and sidewalks connecting the homes together. I loved the sidewalks because they were often filled with couples walking, or precious children riding their bikes and scooters. So after months of prayer, we decided to purchase it.

My favorite part of the lot was a gorgeous oak tree in the middle of what would soon be our backyard. Its massive trunk measured five feet in diameter. I imagined it with a tire swing and many future picnics underneath the canopy of its branches.

Unfortunately, a few days after we purchased the lot, there was a storm. And would you believe that beautiful, magnificent tree split right in two? It collapsed to the ground! It shattered because it was hollow inside. Obviously, the trunk was rotten and had eroded; therefore, the core was not healthy enough to provide nourishment to the other rings. This is why the outwardly beautiful tree had fallen . . . with a hard crash.

Sometimes we see this exact storyline in people's lives. They encounter a storm and believe they have no internal substance, they are unable to stand up under the pressure, and they experience a great fall. Now this can seem confusing to those without discernment, because from the outside, everything appears bold and beautiful. But those who understand God's principles realize this person was not making choose-life choices, so their trunk was unhealthy and hollow. They had been void of God's substance all along.

Proverbs 25:28 says, "like a city whose walls are broken through is a person who lacks self-control." There is a powerful revelation in this Proverb. It shows us that ruling and governing our spirit well keeps us safe and protected. So in this instance, we must saturate our core with the substance of God. This will assure we don't live life from an empty center. It is true that through our born-again spirit, we possess inside of us everything we need that pertains to life and godliness. So we are without excuse. Our aspiration is for our union with God to overflow, and then, dominate our Self, our soul, and our body rings.

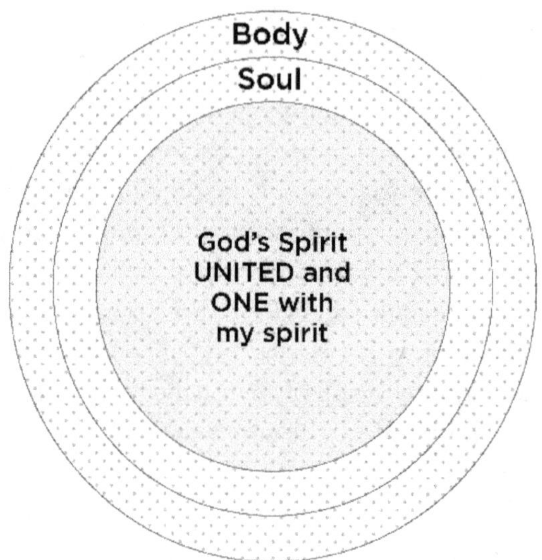

[Figure G—God's Spirit/your spirit man overflowing and dominating your Self ring]

**Note: The little dots are symbolic of God's Spirit overflowing out of your core into your Self (Soul and Body) ring.*

MY FIRST TWENTY YEARS OF SELF

My childhood was filled with brokenness, which naturally meant I had an unhealthy trunk. I was an unplanned pregnancy. My parents were struggling individually and as a couple. They were in the process of separating when my mom realized she was pregnant with me. They tried to make it work, but things seemed to escalate from bad to worse. Before I was two years old, my parents divorced. Throughout my foundational years, I was told by my older siblings that "you are a mistake," "they didn't even want you," and "you caused the divorce," etc.... *Now, as an adult, I realize they were just trying to make sense and find a cause for the brokenness around them.*

Unfortunately, my parents fought constantly and often communicated through screaming or cold-shouldering each other. All the while my older sister, brother and I were shuffled back and forth from house to house. By the time I was in seventh grade, my mom and dad had each married two more times to other people.

After my sixth-grade year, I wanted to be closer to my sister and brother, so I decided to move into my dad's house where they were living. The house was always busy and swirling with something new—at times there were nine kids all under one roof, between the full, half-, and step-siblings. Although, many people in the same house surrounded me, the message was planted deep in my soul that "I am alone" and "nobody gets me." For years I struggled with rejection.

As I began to know Jesus in a personal way, it was important for His truth to flood into me. This veracity needed to overcome every part of my thoughts, feelings, wounds, inner vows and desires. I knew I needed to make agreements with God and His Word regarding my identity, my story, and me. Otherwise, one day, my life would fall with a hard crash, just like the tree in the lot that we had purchased. During this process, I *had* to discover my true Self, the one God created, not the one declared by others. And discover it I *did*!

BECOMING YOUR TRUE SELF

Now, before each of us was born, God had in mind the person He created us to be. He dreamed about the life we would live. This is what I call our *true Self.* When we discover this person God intended us to be, we find our identity! And when we live accordingly, deciding to change from the inside out, true transformation and renewal begins. This is what happened to me. I decided, and then *applied* many right choices, which set me on the correct path.

We do not become a new person by simply changing our *external* behavior. It must be a genuine overflow from our core. For me, habitually making choose-life choices, *out* of my *love* for God, is a lifelong commitment, because I do not want a hollow trunk.

TRUE TRANSFORMATION FROM THE INSIDE OUT

Let's use the popular worship song titled, "Holy Spirit" as an example of how true transformation works. Here are some of the lyrics:

"Holy Spirit, You are welcome here
Come flood this place and fill the atmosphere
Your Glory God is what our hearts long for
To be overcome by Your Presence, Lord . . .
. . . Let us become more aware of Your Presence
Let us experience the Glory of Your Goodness."

Publishing: © 2011 Bryan & Katie Torwalt (ASCAP)
(All rights adm. by Jesus Culture Music)
Produced by Ian Eskelin
Writer(s): Brian & Katie Torwalt

It seems that when people sing this song, they often refer to God's Spirit flooding the *external* space around them—the room, the building. They often rehearse these words to God, requesting His heavy-weighted glory (*kabod*) fall upon the *physical* space. This is good, but what if their appeal was for His Spirit to fill their *internal* space? What if He consumed their Self—mind, will, emotions and body? What if every time they sang the words, they pictured their core overflowing with His glory? Would this not be transformative? What if they visualized His Presence exploding from the inside out?

This shift in mindset would change the world! Don't stop here, because it's not only about the visualization, but the application. It's about assessing, aligning, and governing our inner world with God's Word in these moments. We must have godly character. When we have inner virtue, our life will reflect His glory. Too many Christians live their lives wanting God to show up on the outside, but God is after an internal change—pure motives, and a pure heart. This is the fear of the Lord in action, or the beginning of wisdom, because we stop ordering our lives according to what pleases people and start living and stewarding our Self by what honors God.

OVERCOMING IN LIFE

I have noticed there seems to be "a gap" in many Christians' lives. It is the space between possessing the ability to overcome versus *actually* overcoming. And the internal/external mentality we just read about is probably to blame.

Overcomers have a different focus; they put God first in everything. They face challenges without bowing to the flesh, they possess a trust in God that astounds even the wise. And they do these feats because they have learned Who God is for them. They don't just have relationship with God; they have fellowship with Him. They are normal, average people, except for the fact they have paid the price to know Him personally. They have forsaken all others for this one thing—to walk intimately with God.

These are the ones He longs to showcase to the world, the ones that creation has been waiting to see revealed. They are the *overcomers, the sons and daughters of God*!

"For creation waits in eager expectation for the children (sons and daughters) of God to be revealed."
Rom. 8:19

These are those who seek Him fervently, and consequently, grow tall and strong, even in the winds of adversity. They allow God to dominate their trunk, which spills over into their soul. The spiritual saturation of their mind, will, and emotions is *not* an option, as it causes them to cease being led by secular desires. They are committed to make continual choose-life choices, increasing their spirit into their soul, so that all carnal tendencies are snuffed out, because *those* desires reap nothing but death. Overcomers will continue to bear beautiful fruit, no matter the season.

Possessing these mindsets is how we "close the gap" and experience Jesus' abundant Zoë Life. They are key choose-life attitudes, which continually feed and increase God's Spirit in our core and cause us to yield to His voice. When we yield (surrender) to Him, we yield (produce) great fruit.

THE SURRENDERED, TRUSTED LIFE

Overcoming in life is also about surrendering, and saying "Yes!" to Jesus, every day in many, mini situations and circumstances. It is telling Him, "I believe You are good. I believe you are *for* me. So even though I can't understand what is going on, I trust You. You know what is best for me. I want You to be in charge."

Overcoming in life is allowing His Spirit to cross the boundary lines of our core and inundate us with *His* thoughts, ways, words, desires, and emotions. Then, as we make further choose-life choices, His Spirit and His love are released into our next ring. This is how we grow up and mature. This is how we govern our Self and develop a healthy trunk.

We can experience the fire and passion of God to such a degree that all desires for old habits and lusts disappear. We will experience The Zoë Life of peace and joy, to the degree that we submit each part of our Self (thoughts, emotions, desires, habits, impurities, plans, dreams, and body) to His ways. We limit God by not allowing Him to dominate our soul and body. We limit God by not saying "Yes" continually and consistently to Him. We limit God *when we choose* not to receive Him into every part of our being.

Those who have been betrayed and tested in the fires of adversity are willing to yield and surrender to Jesus, and they are now being raised up in God's resurrection power. It is *your choice* to reveal your true Self, every part of you—spirit, soul, and body, by learning to live in the realm of the Spirit.

"For those who are led by the Spirit of God,
these are the sons and daughters of God."
Rom. 8:14

Now is the time . . .

Your Tree Growing: Overcoming Little by Little

Many people struggle with becoming "an overcomer." I did for years. Even though I had sincerely surrendered to Jesus, and I was a new creation, I was confused as to why I didn't see immediate change. At the time, I didn't realize transformation is a lifelong journey. And many times, overcoming happens little by little. I learned the importance of my agreements with what God says of me. My daily "Yeses!" to Jesus caused me to overcome. These decisions allowed me to connect with my true Self and disconnect from the old "autopilot" habits that had been in motion for years.

LITTLE BY LITTLE

Growing up, my family of origin was plagued with abuse and addiction (alcohol, drugs, and sex). I saw the fierce grip it had on them, and I wanted the generational cycles broken in my life. So I was determined to never drink, do drugs or be promiscuous. Yet I didn't know how to deal with pain and brokenness in a healthy manner. It wasn't until I was born-again that my eyes were open to an addiction that I had. It was food.

I can't recall when my struggle with overeating began. It may have originated at an early age when our pantry was often empty, and I was hungry. Because of those times, maybe I developed a poverty-mindset, feeling like I didn't have enough, so I "stored up." Or perhaps, when there were shelves full of groceries, I would overeat in order to feel full and provided for. Nevertheless, somewhere along the way, as I walked through painful moments and seasons, I became emotionally tied to food. My internal pain manifested in a physical way.

When I began walking with Jesus intimately, I felt the conviction of not using food for its original intention, which was delicious *fuel* for my body. I realized I had been using it to soothe the heartaches of life. Sometimes, I would eat out of boredom, loneliness, rejection or insecurity. Other times, I would eat to *dodge* taking the right steps to move me forward. I didn't realize I was self-sabotaging because the food caused me to "feel something different" than the pain. The overeating numbed my hurt, and gave me a sense of *control.* I knew it would give me momentary satisfaction. I tried sharing with my parents that I struggled with overeating, but since I wasn't overweight, nor was I anorexic or bulimic, they didn't take me seriously. Because I played college soccer, they assumed I must need all the extra helpings.

In reality, I lacked self-control to stop using food to "scratch the itch" of the ache in my heart. But it all came to light during my junior year in college, when I suffered a hip fracture while playing soccer. I considered the whole ordeal a blessing from God. Because I was on crutches for six weeks, all the inactivity coupled with overeating caused me to gain weight quickly. It was then my family was able to recognize my struggle with food.

Certain family members and friends showed me compassion during that season and I was very thankful. With their love and encouragement, I began making more choose-life choices. I moved from living a food-focused "quick-fix high" to a Jesus-lasting solution. Little by little, Deuteronomy 30:19 became alive in me. Day by day, I learned *how* to choose life by saturating my Self with God's Spirit. I had to stay *connected* to His Spirit inside of me, by recognizing His promptings and nudges. I was slowly learning how to overcome.

If you find yourself in any kind of struggle of addiction, remember the keys that helped me: Stay connected to God. Choose to live by His Word, stop seeking quick fixes and replace them with His Presence through worship or prayer. When we are in God's manifested Presence, we are changed into His likeness. Chains fall off, strongholds are broken, and diseases are healed. So consider making your personal time with Jesus your only addiction.

REPLACING MY THOUGHTS: THE MIND

Gradually, I was doing the hard work of renewing my mind with God's truth. I was learning *how* to command my thoughts and attention to remain fixed on Him. I was learning to see myself as He sees me. And I learned how to agree with God and His Word about my extraordinary "new nature." The zoë fullness is about believing and receiving the oneness we share with Jesus. We share His exact DNA! When we choose to believe and receive the fullness of our identity, offered through Jesus, God's Spirit floods us. I was beginning to understand I am everything Jesus *is* and nothing He is *not*; Jesus is a King, so I am royalty. Jesus has authority, so I have authority. Jesus is holy, so I am holy. Jesus is beautiful, so I am beautiful. Jesus is wealthy, so I am wealthy. The fullness of God dwells in Jesus, so the fullness of God dwells in me. Agreeing with God's truth, again and again, in my thoughts no matter the circumstance, was key to allowing His Spirit to saturate my Self. This is how I received Jesus into every part of me. This is daily believing and receiving Him *fully*. This is a choose-life choice.

REPLACING SELFISH DESIRES: THE WILL

Many of us have read Proverbs 3:5–6, which says, "Trust in the Lord with all your heart and lean not on your own understanding; in all your ways acknowledge Him, and He will direct your paths."

This is how I began changing my desires: in *all* things, I replaced my will with God's will. Daily, I chose to not make my own choices, but instead, I ask Jesus to direct my decisions. And God began to take territory on the inside. I had to stay in continual conversation with Jesus, which is key to living as an overcomer.

As I continued to say, "Yes!" to Him and surrender to His Spirit, the old sins fell off, effortlessly. The more space *God* consumes, the less space there is for the "sins of Self": selfishness, self-pity, self-indulgence, self-protection, self-centeredness, self-focus, self-hatred or self-sabotage. This is a choose-life choice.

REPLACING SOULISH FEELINGS: THE EMOTIONS

Overcomers live with God's peace, joy, and hope, without changing the past. They refuse to be snagged emotionally. They have learned not to struggle with intimidation, worry, anxiety, depression, hopelessness, confusion, and fear. Additionally, they navigate through any insecurity, shame, guilt or blame by *receiving* Jesus' healing touch in these wounds. When it concerns past situations and people, they open up their heart to God, and allow Him to speak *truth*, so they can become whole and healed. It is imperative they see life through a healthy emotional lens.

Little by little, and by God's grace, I have learned how to replace my past emotions with His truth, so that I am no longer stuck in old feelings of pain. I did this by saying additional "Yeses" to Jesus, by revisiting any difficult situation, while in the Presence of God. It is here, that He touched every part of my story. If ever I do feel "triggered," I continue to move forward by presenting the situation and myself to Him for His perspective and truth.

In this special time, I press into His Spirit and ask for a new branding, until I feel a release inside of me. This has become my habit instead of reaching for food, or any other substance. I can literally feel God's Spirit *advancing* within me, leaving His emotional climate of peace, ease, humility, contentment and thanksgiving. Always before me is the choice to usher in God's Spirit fully, to penetrate my emotions. Receiving and agreeing with the way God feels about things is how I experience His zoë, abundance. This is a choose-life choice.

OVERCOMING TRAUMA

Many people suffer from some sort of trauma, whether it is from divorce, abuse, serving in the military, or another cause. There are many awful things people suffer these days all over the world. If these traumas are not dealt with properly, they can leave your soul living from a place of "survival," which will lead to a life of chaos. Very few ever recover from a life of chaos without outside help. This could be the reason there are so many homeless and helpless in our land. The first way to overcome any trauma is to establish a disciplined daily routine, such as applying the choose-life decisions. This will produce a *stability* that will allow your life to heal. But it will take time. I cannot emphasize enough how much following God produces *stability* in a life that has been traumatized.

GOD'S SPIRIT MUST OVERFLOW INTO THE BODY

The search for gratification can lead to a host of obsessions. The use of painkillers has become an epidemic. And our culture is a greenhouse for growing addictions through our physical senses. For instance, I have a friend who claims to have seen every Netflix series. Another friend can't stop getting tattoos. Still yet, another keeps overdoing it in tanning beds, while another has spent thousands of dollars on plastic surgery. A young girl is exceptionally bright and has a great personality yet has been fired from several jobs because she can't unplug from knowing what her friends are doing on social media while she is working. Recently, a physician at our local hospital quit his job because he didn't want to give up his addiction to video games. He spent hours every night playing them, and finally, the lack of sleep and poor work ethic caught up. The stimulation, or the temporary high, overcame his body.

THE GATE

The body is "the gate" in which the soul tries to find satisfaction. This is how addictions happen. People use alcohol, sex, social media, video games, pornography, drugs, excessive shopping or hobbies, food and more. In actuality, their emotions, thoughts, and desires are wounded, and thereby captured by demonic influences. But there is only one way out, God can satisfy the soul thirst. It is only through the saturation of His Spirit, which overflows from the core, that will satiate the soul pain and solve the ferocious cravings of the body.

Now, if a new Christian were to continue to "reach and grab" the things of this world with their body, it would actually combat the renewal process. So there must be continuous, deliberate, choose-life choices made daily, in order for the Spirit to have more influence in their Self. Living with a connection to Jesus must be constant, and then overcoming will happen effortlessly—"not by might nor by power but by God's Spirit." (Zech. 4:6)

This will release a genuine zoë, freedom and breakthrough. All old patterns will lose their grip and be replaced. Some people may have a prodigal son experience (Luke 15:17) where they "come to their senses." But it's important for us *all* to live according to Mark 8:36 which says, "For what shall it profit a man to gain the whole world, and forfeit his life [in the eternal kingdom of God]? (AMP)"

God's dream for our lives is that Jesus will radiate in every part of us. As He saturates our Self, we become healthy, whole, and complete. These sons and daughters, *the Overcomers*, will not leave creation waiting; they will rise up and express God's wonder and majesty! They will live as we are destined to live, with a "healthy trunk," full of life and substance—*Jesus*, in their soul and body. *Christ in us* is the hope of glory! (Col. 1:27)

"But the time is coming and is already here,
when by the power of God's Spirit,
people will worship the Father as He really is,
offering Him the true worship that He wants."
John 4:23

Now is the time . . .

Your Tree's Fragrance: Atmosphere & Domains

She is captivating—both inside and out! It's obvious that the beauty overflows from her core. She lights up the room everywhere she goes. People can't help but notice when she arrives, because her presence causes a shift in the atmosphere.

I'm not talking about her style or the clothes she wears. It's her radiance that grabs everyone's attention. It is almost like she shines brighter than everyone else. Her eyes sparkle when she smiles. Her countenance seems to glow, as she wears pleasantness upon her face. Her words are full of praise, encouragement, and thanksgiving.

If you stand anywhere near her, she will most likely hug you, or lovingly touch you, or perhaps, she will give you an invitational glance. She wants to let you know you are seen and allowed to join her conversation or space. Her warm affection makes everyone feel known, loved, and "welcomed here." No matter where she goes, she spreads energy, joy, and delight with whomever she encounters. It doesn't matter if you're the grocery store clerk, or a waiter, you will feel love overflowing out of her. When I am with her, the atmosphere she carries causes me to think about Jesus.

What I just described is a woman who *sets* atmospheres through what she cultivates internally. It's a phenomenal concept, really. And if you peer beyond the walls of this room, likely you'll find an entire community affected by this woman's life choices. It is the same for us. Our internal decisions not only impact our personal well-being, but they have a spillover effect upon the world around us.

[Figure H—God's Spirit is taking more territory, flooding into the Atmosphere ring and creating a "fragrance" for others]

Once God's Spirit dominates your Self ring, you can begin to take territory in the atmosphere ring. The atmosphere you carry is incredibly powerful. It's the verbal and nonverbal "deposits" or "withdrawals" you make in a space that affect others. For instance, take Peter's shadow (Acts 5:15–16); it healed the sick and delivered those tormented by evil spirits. Everywhere Peter walked, the atmosphere and the people were changed.

Imagine that being you!

The atmosphere we offer others can *positively* or *negatively* influence their life. When we are saturated by God's Spirit, it's easy to provide a healthy environment for others to blossom and flourish. You can't force people to choose life, but you can provide an atmosphere and an invitation that is full of life (zoë). This will make it easier for people to connect with God's original design for them. Envision yourself carrying the atmosphere of Heaven throughout your day. Every time you interact with someone, they will experience a bit of God, of His goodness and glory.

You will recognize them by their fruit.
Grapes aren't gathered from thorn bushes or figs from thistles, are they?
Even so, every good tree produces good fruit,
But the rotten tree produces bad fruit.
A good tree cannot produce bad fruit,
Nor can a rotten tree produce good fruit.
Matt. 7:16–18

CONTRASTING ATMOSPHERES

Heaven and Hell have very specific atmospheres. The atmosphere of Heaven is: healthy, kind, honoring, patient, joyful, wise, hopeful, celebratory, thankful, generous, peaceful, beautiful, faithful, honest, full of praise, full of trust, orderly, flexible, persevering, easy, lighthearted, smiling, restful, self-restraining, optimistic, graceful, merciful, purposeful, mighty, abundant, pure, exciting, enduring, inclusive, whimsical, good, and life-giving.

The atmosphere of Hell is: stressed, stoic, lacking, lonely, worried, frustrated, irritated, demanding, agitated, diminishing, gossiping, prideful, diseased, bitter, malignant, fearful, stingy, unforgiving, resentful, intolerant, raging, pessimistic, depressed, impatient, hateful, vicious, mean, abusive, fake, betraying, insensitive, hard-hearted, unfeeling, powerless, hopeless, sarcastic, lacking, uncaring, iron-fisted, rigid, sharp, rude, exclusive, inconsiderate, disagreeable, disharmonious, and death-producing.

Every person exudes an atmosphere that resembles either Heaven or Hell. And every time someone enters that space, there is a Heaven or Hell *shift* in the room. So now is the time to make sure Jesus' nature, (or the environment of Heaven) is yours.

Right now, pause; turn off your phone and any other distractions. Become quiet and still. Close your eyes so you can focus on hearing and seeing with your spirit. Turn your palms face up and posture your body to receive, as you present yourself to the Lord. Ask God, "What atmosphere do I carry?" Let Him examine your heart, as you envision yourself dialoguing with people at work. Now, revisit your conversations at home. What does He show you? Do not be defensive. Allow Him to reveal what *He* sees.

Do you need to make any changes?
If so, simply say, "Yes!" Agree with Him.
Simply choose life.
You have the freedom to choose.

YOUR TREE'S FRAGRANCE

Your tree has a fragrance that overflows outwardly from the health of your trunk. Fragrance doesn't focus on behavior modification, or external change. It is a *by-product* of the atmosphere you carry. As we discussed, it is the *governing*, the *stewarding*, of the core and Self rings that produce any outward results. Here are a few questions to ask yourself to help you assess the fragrance of your tree:

- Do you project a stoic and icy atmosphere, or does your presence bring warmth and honor?

- Do you offer others demands and irritation or thankfulness and grace?
- Is your home a place of order and peace, or chaos and stress?
- Do you offer relaxation and rejuvenation, or isolation and loneliness?

"Let me tell you why you are here.
You're here to be salt-seasoning that brings
out the God-flavors of this earth.
If you lose your saltiness, how will people taste godliness?
You've lost your usefulness and will end up in the garage.
Here's another way to put it:
You're here to be light bringing out the God-colors in the world.
God is not a secret to be kept.
We're going public with this, as public as a city on a hill.
Keep open house,
be generous with your lives.
By opening up to others,
you'll prompt people to open up with God,
this generous Father in Heaven."
Matt. 5:13
The Message

A BLESSING PRAYER FOR YOU

May you use your freedom to choose to connect
to God's Spirit in your core.
May you operate in the authority that Jesus has given you.
May you choose to live your life by carrying His anointing
that quickens, arouses, and awakens people to connect with
His presence.
May the abundant, zoë goodness of God fill you,
and those around you.
In Jesus name, amen.

Now is the time . . .

With this Ring, I Thee Wed: Marriage

The cries from my six-week-old baby startled me. My heart began to race. It was early in the morning and still dark outside. I stumbled down the hall half-asleep and opened the door to her room. Everything was fine, she was just reminding me it was time for her 3:00 a.m. feeding.

After her little tummy was full, she fell back to sleep. I decided to stay up and enjoy the quiet time praying and reading, before my two toddlers awoke for the day. I opened the Bible to Matthew 13. I've read the Parable of the Sower many times, but this morning was unique. As I sat there, meditating on what God was writing upon my heart, my husband entered the room.

"Good morning," I said with a smile.

"Good morning to you."

"What are you doing up so early?" I inquired.

He responded, "I heard you get up with the baby and then I couldn't get back to sleep, so I decided to read."

"Oh, what are you reading?" I asked.

"Matthew 13," he replied.

I looked at him, amazed. "That's awesome! That's what I read! I don't think that has ever happened before—reading the same passage of the Bible on the same morning, without trying. This is exciting. It sounds like the Holy Spirit is up to something. What popped out at you? What do you think He is highlighting?"

He chuckled at my early morning perkiness, "Yes, it is really special. I don't recall it happening before either. God revealed something new to me about the parable of the sower. Why do you think He would choose to order the words in verse eight this way, 'produced a crop—a hundred, sixty or thirty times what was sown'?"

I reread the parable focusing on verse 8, and then, I quickly realized the same word order happened a *second* time in verse 23. I sat back, in awe. The revelation grabbed my heart. We don't speak like this! I believe we would say our numbers in increasing order, or in different multiples of each other, so that they are congruent. For instance, "thirty, sixty, and ninety," not "thirty, sixty, and *hundred*."

Yet Jesus started with *hundredfold* twice!

I have always appreciated and respected God's intentionality. And *this* morning, it left me in wonder. I could feel the thickness of the Holy Spirit in the room, as I prayed for full understanding of what He had for me, for my husband, for us all. Throughout the parable He says, "He who has ears let them hear." I believe God was revealing it's the condition of the heart that determines the level of harvest a person receives from the Word sown.

Right then, I began asking God, "May I live a life that bears fruit a hundredfold! May I share with others how to live a 'hundredfold life of fruitfulness'! May Your people never settle for sixty or thirtyfold. May we live lives of faith, leaning into *all* that You are offering."

I could feel my heart burning. And since then, I have continued to pray this prayer for myself, my husband, our children, our family, our friends, for pastors, mentors, government leaders, and more. I want everyone to experience the hundredfold life, in each ring! I constantly ask God to open our eyes that we may see what He is doing; to open our ears that we may hear what He is saying; and to open our hearts that we may understand.

As we see, hear, and understand, we must *choose to change,* so we can have maximum fruitfulness. *Unfortunately, once we become Christians, many of us do not mind the thirtyfold or sixtyfold fruitful life.* But God's original idea was for us to possess the full abundance Jesus came to bring. He has many upgrades for us once we become born again.

This is the pursuit He has designated for us to chase. And this quest starts in the realm of expectation! We must think His thoughts toward ourselves. We must exchange our wants for His plenty and our poverty for His abundance. This is His dream for us. This is the "Great Exchange." This is why Jesus came to earth. This is why God listed the order of numbers the way He did, to receive the hundredfold blessing every time. And this every time includes the ring of marriage!

TWO BECOMING ONE

I believe God's abundant fruitfulness in the Marriage ring looks like both spouses who are head-over-heels in love with Jesus (true layed-down lovers of Him), running alongside each other with the same cadence, hand-in-hand on the choose-life path. These souls possess the same eternal vision and goals, and they are true teammates. They have an understanding for each other's hearts and minds in a deep way. They are truly best friends, always treating each other with much love, kindness, appreciation, and honor.

This is God's best for all marriages. But for some, the pathway to this hundredfold blessing may look a little different than one might expect. Some marriages might start off having to trudge through challenges and difficulties, until they reach the greater outcome. And others, who have had extreme hardships, may be tempted to settle for the thirty, or sixtyfold blessing. But perhaps it is the marriages that have *learned to love* that hold the greatest value.

Throughout the Bible, the greatest lesson is *learning to love*. According to 1 Corinthians 13, we could give everything we own to the poor and even go to the stake to be burned, but if we don't love, we have gained nothing.

Marriage is a beautiful institution for cultivating this principle. There is nothing like it. It is uniquely designed to receive many blessings, through the process of refinement. According to John 15:2, when we undergo pruning, we become more fruitful.

"He cuts off every branch in me that bears no fruit,
while every branch that does bear fruit,
He prunes so that it will be even more fruitful."
John 15:2

So when we choose to embrace painful moments in our marriage versus dodging, deflecting, or complaining, we can position ourselves to bear a hundredfold fruit in our Marriage ring, not just sixty or thirty. God can use difficult circumstances to remove things that do not belong in our long-term story.

Pruning may feel like many, *mini-deaths*, because that is exactly what is happening. Yet like John 12:24 says, "when there is death, there is also life." The pruning can advance God's glory and goodness into every part of our Marriage ring, if we submit to the process. Pruning is necessary for connecting to God's hundredfold zoë fruitfulness.

Our part is to continue to choose life by showering our spouse with love, as well as being thankful and rejoicing. Our part is to measure and judge ourselves, to check *our* motives and actions before the Lord, making sure we are rightly loving our spouse. We should never let our spouse's behavior and attitude determine how well we love them. God is our Judge, determining whether or not we are learning to love.

[Figure I—God's Spirit taking more territory, overflowing into the Marriage ring]

"Two are better than one,
Because they get a good return for their effort.
For if one falls,
The other one will lift up his companion."
Ecc. 4:9–10

I love this verse for marriages. It is a valuable reminder of the power in numbers. Unfortunately, not every marriage takes advantage of this opportunity. For many marriages, when one falls, the other isn't there to lift up their companion. So often, we accuse and judge the other when they stumble. We say, "How could you have done this to me?" or "What is wrong with you?"

Each day we have many, mini-opportunities to align our thoughts, emotions, and desires with God; embrace His divine pruning process; and commit to learning to love and honor our spouse deeply. Begin making the necessary choose-life choices today to experience a life that produces a hundred-fold return in your marriage. Stay connected to God's Spirit within you, so that you overflow with His love and direction for your spouse.

Now is the time . . .

Blessed with Branches: Children

I was driving my minivan through town with my three daughters in the backseat. We were having a casual conversation, when my middle daughter, who was four-years-old at the time, said, "Mommy, you need to be very careful with me."

"Well, yes, you are right, honey. I do need to treat you with care. What brought that to mind?" I smiled.

She said, "I was just thinking that *I am God's,* and if you aren't careful with me, He will not like that. He wants you to take good care of me."

I encouraged her, "Yes, sweetheart, you are right! You are *His*! He loves you, cares for you and is watching over you. It matters greatly to Him how you are treated and cared for!"

Her words brought a smile to my heart and face. As a parent, I don't know if there is any greater joy than witnessing your child's heart and mind being utterly convinced that they are God's treasure, and He deeply loves them! I was amazed that at her young age, she understood she belonged to Him more than to me. She knew it is important to *Him* that she is treated well. Her heart was convinced that she is a gift from God, and I had been entrusted to steward it wisely.

PARENTS CAN BE GENERATION-CHANGERS

There are thousands of parenting books with endless suggestions on how to raise your children. This brief chapter isn't supposed to be a comprehensive guide on how to parent. I am simply focusing on a few key ways to allow God's Spirit to advance and take territory in our Children ring.

One of my favorite things about being a parent is the opportunity to be a generation-changer. This truth might sound overwhelming. But the reality is, by simply evaluating the choices our parents made raising us, we can determine if we want to continue, or change the legacy through our own decisions. We get to decide what kind of mom or dad we would like to be. Hopefully, we will create an upgraded vision for our future generations. Proverbs 29:18 says it well, "where there is no vision, the people perish." One intentional decision can have a great impact. It can affect the health and wellness of the next generation.

Recently, I was speaking to a gentleman in his seventies. He shared his story of growing up, and how he went to thirteen elementary schools in six years. He didn't want his children to experience the same unstable upbringing during their foundational years. His hope was to offer them a secure and stable upbringing. He wanted them to feel rooted and grounded, with strong friendships and connections. So his vision was to stay in the same house until all his children were adults. This one decision brought an upgrade to his next generation.

In my foundational years, one of my parents was physically abusive. (Unfortunately, they had experienced this behavior as a child too.) Although I was the youngest child in the family, I recall times I would stand in front of my older sister and brother, to protect them from physical and verbal rage.

Also, I remember seeing my grandmother be physically and verbally abusive. One morning, I walked into her kitchen, as she grabbed the back of my aunt's hair and slammed her head against the kitchen counter. The reason: my aunt did not load the dishwasher correctly. Even though I was young, I felt deep sadness and compassion, realizing the environment and behavior with which my parent was most likely raised.

Another parent struggled with alcoholism and smoking pot every day. Both of these addictions had a tight grip. Throughout my entire upbringing, that parent never overcame the stronghold of these substances. I never knew my dad sober and healthy. He died prematurely.

As a generation-changer (ahem, I mean a parent), we should assess any addictions, poor habits, or lies our parents believed or are still involved in. We have the power and authority to do the work and make the changes in our stories, so our children can have a brighter legacy. Our decisions will greatly affect the fruitfulness of the next generation. As a generation-changer, every breakthrough we set in motion will be a step forward for our children. For me, the greatest thing we can teach our children is how to love and forgive—not only others, but also themselves. Helping them see life through the lens of loving and forgiveness is a legacy I will never regret.

SMALL DECISION, GREAT IMPACT

Another intentional decision I am choosing to make is "guarding family time," specifically the time together at the dinner table. Growing up, we didn't own a table large enough for us all to sit and eat together. The food would be in the kitchen for each person to come whenever they wanted and make their meal. Some family members would sit in front of the television to eat, while others took their plate outside, or to their bedroom.

Research shows that the health and well-being of a child can stem from family dinnertime. I want to offer that beautiful opportunity. The vision is to gather around the table, together as a family, looking into each other's eyes, and truly getting to know each other. It's a time to offer encouragement, and to listen. Many things surface during mealtimes because it is a comfortable environment to reach out. (I understand that as my children age, it will be more difficult to guard these special moments at the table. So I've intentionally started while they are young.)

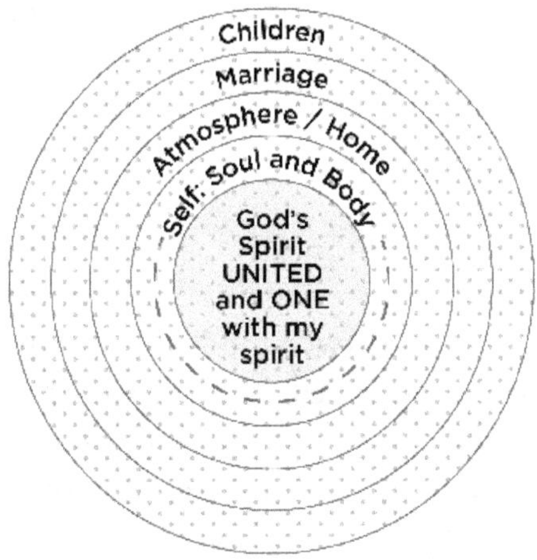

[Figure J—God's Spirit advancing and overflowing into the Children ring]

EQUIPPING

Finally, probably the most important lesson we can offer our children is to help them discover how to connect with God's glory and goodness. It is critical they learn how to present themselves to God and also know how to stay connected to Him. This will empower them to overcome temptations, negative emotions, and to make choose-life choices. The hundredfold zoë fruitfulness of this ring also teaches our children how to take ownership for their decisions. They must say, "Yes!" to Jesus for themselves, and learn how to take personal responsibility, especially in relationships. It is surprising how difficult it is for some adults (because they never learned as children) to simply address their mistake, apologize, and ask forgiveness. This is a critical step to "growing up" and living healthy, with *zoë-full* abundance.

It may feel daunting to equip them in this manner. But it's imperative they learn at a young age, how to listen to His Spirit within their core, how to saturate their Self with Him, and how to allow His nature to overflow into their atmosphere. We must help them learn how to increase His Spirit with the many, mini-choices (or deaths) they will have each day.

THREE TOP KEYS

The three keys to mastering this challenging task: Number one, model it; number two, model it; and number three, model it. Our children need to see what it looks like to be head-over-heels in love with Jesus. The best lessons are more "caught" than taught, and this is especially true for parenting. Modeling will always be more effective than telling.

Living each day undone by God's loving kindness, while overflowing with gratitude toward Him, qualifies you to tell your kids, "follow me" or "watch how I do it." They need to observe you reading your Bible and being still before the Lord. They need to regularly watch you lingering in His presence until you hear His voice in your core. They need to observe you worshiping freely—expressing creativity, and obeying God's leading and nudges. I believe if our children watch us live our lives daily, choosing to be Spirit-led, it will help them connect to being God's mature sons and daughters too. After all, God doesn't have grandchildren.

"Train up a child in the way he should go,
and even when he is old, he will not depart from it."
Prov. 22:6

Of course, the best time to start this training for growth and success is when they are toddlers. Yet it is never too late to implement choose-life choices. There's a popular Chinese proverb that says, "The best time to plant a tree was twenty years ago. The second-best time is *now*."

Now is the time . . .

In this Family Ring, "I Belong!": Team

It had been a long weekend.

My body was achy and tired. I traveled out of state with my competitive soccer team and stayed with the family of one of my teammates. My family couldn't afford to travel to out of state tournaments. Not only because of the financial cost, but because they needed to be available locally to transport my siblings to their activities.

By the time I arrived home on Sunday evening, it was late.

As soon as I opened the door, I could sense the atmosphere was different, almost eerie. There were only a few of my siblings in the living room.

Very gingerly, I asked, "What is going on?"

Their heads were hanging low. They were all quiet for a long time. Then my sister glanced up at me. She shared that our twenty-year-old brother had committed suicide.

Immediately, I felt the pain in my gut and dropped to the floor. I looked up at my father with silent desperation and hopelessness.

The next couple of days were foggy, but the feelings of those days were branded in my memory.

We still went to school that week, but I couldn't hear what the teachers were saying to me. I'll never forget that September. It was my junior year of high school, and I had just turned sixteen. My classmates were eager with excitement for the start of a new year. But I couldn't relate. I felt like time had stopped. Attending school was difficult, but being at the house was even more challenging.

As the months progressed, things seemed to spiral. And for years my family struggled with healing. Holidays and celebrations were particularly hard. The pain was loud and seemed unquenchable. Every one of us experienced brokenness. We needed great repairing. The family members, who felt overlooked, discounted, or diminished, were now experiencing those emotions to a greater degree. We didn't know it then, but we needed Jesus. We needed His healing touch.

Oh, how I wish I could turn back the hands of time! I wish we could've all been together, as a powerful team, standing in a circle and holding hands. Each person could face inward, toward one another, while every family member took turns telling those standing near or beside them:

"God loves you so much!"
"I love you!"
"You matter!"
"You are made for a special reason!"
"How can I best celebrate and encourage you?"
"I love seeing you use your gifts and talents!"
and finally, "You belong!"

This is the truth of what God thought about each of us! But at the time, we did not know His Zoë Life existed. I realize the hardship was not God's original intention, and it was very sad to watch my family suffer so much. But I am thankful

God has healed my heart. And I am restored *only* because I allowed Him in, and I *chose* His way of life over my own.

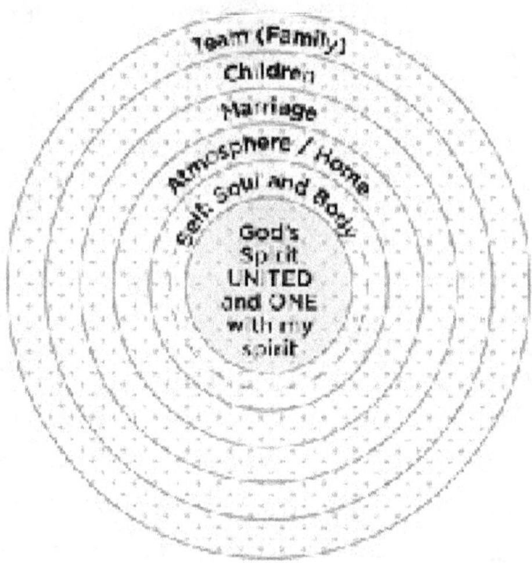

[Figure K—God's Spirit overflowing from the core and saturating the Team ring]

THE TEAM

After you've discovered the fruitfulness of how being in love with Jesus affects your atmosphere, your marriage and your children, it is time to experience God's Spirit overflow into your Team ring. The Team ring has its own identity. It is comprised of each family member, collectively. Now, the happiest families are a team. They know each one has a divine purpose and calling to fulfill. They may become frustrated at times but in order to stay a team they work through difficulties and try it again. They communicate to one another by actions, words, and deeds: "You belong here." And belonging sends the message, "You are loved."

It's important each teammate knows he (or she) doesn't need to compete with another's ability, as each is gifted individually. Jealousy has no place here. One teammate's talents and giftings do not need to reflect another teammate's talents and giftings. Everyone has permission to excel in who they were created to be. Each teammate loves celebrating and championing one another. They love seeing one another shine and overcome challenges. Each teammate knows he belongs and is confident that without his position and contribution, the team wouldn't radiate God's glory and goodness as beautifully. Each player knows they are significant to the team.

"Neither do people light a lamp and put it under a bowl.
Instead they put it on its stand,
and it gives light to everyone in the house.
In the same way, let your light shine before others,
that they may see your good deeds
and glorify your Father in Heaven."
Matt. 5:15–16

When God's Spirit is overflowing into the Team ring, the family is tight and connected. No football program wants all quarterbacks, wide receivers, or linebackers. Their different body types, strengths, weaknesses, and ambitions have value. They actually feel encouraged and supported by each other's abilities; otherwise, they could not win a game. Their bond sends a "we" message to the opposing challenger, and to the world. It is the same with the family unit. If the enemy tries to devour one of the other members, everyone should jump to the occasion and help. We win as a team!

When "belonging" is not found in the family unit, things go awry. It is essential that each team is emotionally available for one another. If we can't rely on our family emotionally, then we will take it upon ourselves to meet our needs in unfulfilled ways. This issue can lead to the attitude that we are "right in our own eyes," and that we don't need our team, which will drive us into isolation. As a result, we will make poor choices and *associate* our identity in performance, perfection, pretending, pleasing, or posing.

YOUR TEAM

There are many options in which you can saturate your team with God's Spirit and influence. Here are a few practical ways to create "team" in your family. One approach is to develop a mission statement that helps everyone understand the collective direction and vision. Here are some examples I have seen: "We will be over the top in love with God and people," "We will value and prioritize family," "We will be in a continual pursuit of learning," "We will strive for excellence in all we do," and "We will be known for our humility and kindness."

Another idea is creating special hand signals or handshakes. My dad had a unique hand signal. Whenever he signaled us, even across the soccer field, we would receive his message of peace and love. Suddenly, I felt, "I am seen, and I belong."

Another inspiration is creating solid routines for how to begin or close each day. Our family has recently begun a morning routine of gathering together in a circle, while holding hands, and choosing to take a physical step forward as a symbolic gesture of each member "stepping into their anointing" for the day.

Still another suggestion is designating special moments for certain days of the week. For example, having pancakes every Saturday morning. Along these lines, one of my favorite ideas is naming each day of the week. This gives every day a special purpose and function (Ex: Thankful Thursday, Family Fun Friday, and Sabbath Sunday). The goal is to be on the same page with the same vision, so that each member knows what it means to be a part of the team. I have done this for years with my family and even when my daughters were young, they knew the focus of the day and enjoyed celebrating it with Zoë Life.

"Then the Lord said, 'Write the vision;
make it plain, so he may run who reads it.'"
Hab. 2:2

There are many creative ways you can send the message to each teammate that "you belong" and "we are together." By championing all their strengths and covering weaknesses, you will empower them to connect with their destiny-story.

THE TABLE

The family table is a unique meeting place of nourishment, connections and fellowship. In many homes, the family table isn't used to its hundredfold abundance. However, if we view it as the control center of the home, abundant fruitfulness within the Team can be accomplished.

One of the greatest assets of each teammate sitting at the table together as a family is the close proximity they have to one another. It could feel awkward and forced for many families to stand in a circle and say, "I love you" or "You belong." But when sitting at the table together, everyone is already physically close, so it becomes easier to connect emotionally and spiritually. Connecting at the table is an easy way to incorporate intimacy with every teammate into the family's daily rhythm.

When we *come to the table*, we have an opportunity to gather as a team and share with one another about the day, but most importantly their value and worth. It can be critical to one's life and destiny to know that their family members believe they are loved, they belong, and are essential to the Team.

When everyone is gathered together closely, try holding hands, and giving God gratitude for His provision of the food and other gifts. After thanking God as a family, this "table time" can be an intentional opportunity to pause and applaud each other's successes or offer comfort in one's mistakes. Take advantage of the moment and look into each other's eyes. Tell one another how special he (or she) is. This is a picture of God's abundant love, His Spirit, overflowing from our core. When we bond with one another *at the table,* we are doing more than just breaking bread, we are taking territory with God's Spirit in our family ring and truly becoming a strong team, to qualify for an undefeated record.

Now is the time . . .

Connecting to the Roots of Others: Your People

God's Spirit advances in this ring when we connect to our People. Your People are usually a group of like-minded individuals running the same direction with you and speaking the same spiritual language. Some may even keep the same cadence! This sect *can* be a person's family, but often it isn't. It's the ones with whom you feel unity, that "one accord" sensation that Jesus prayed for in John 17. It is the ones who truly see you, care for you and encourage you, which cause you to feel known, loved and celebrated.

It is in these relationships that you can most easily be your true self and find acceptance, because these people are *for* you. You can sense it. You are safe with them. They don't diminish your radiance. There is no competition, comparison, or gossip. Instead, you feel their encouragement to put your "light high on a lamp stand for all to see." These types of friendships breed life and freedom, for *your* story, as well as theirs.

Most often, your people will be your brothers and sisters in the Body of Christ. They will be the ones you effortlessly link arms with for spiritual strength and support, as you make strides toward your destiny-story. They won't necessarily hold the answers, or next steps for you, but you won't have to explain yourself to them or justify wholeheartedly seeking after Jesus. It seems God gives them grace to intuitively understand and know you. They will encourage you, cover you in prayer and speak truth into your soul. They will offer exhortation to take another step in the journey, so you can say your next "Yes!" to Jesus.

Sometimes your people can see *how* and *where* God is leading you, even before you can see it yourself. When seasons of discouragement and setbacks come, your people will stick around because they believe your Heaven-story is worth fighting for. Just like Aaron and Hur held up Moses' hands when he was too tired, so they will do for you. (Exod. 17:10–13)

Through the investment of time, conversations, prayer and hope, your people will help you persevere to overcome. They want to see God's dream for you reach the hundredfold fruition! Why? Because it's your destiny-story, the one He created for you before you were born. (Ps. 139:16) The hundredfold life is becoming who God made you to be!

THE REDWOODS

Did you know the Redwood trees located in northern California stand nearly 380+ feet tall but their roots are only five to six feet deep?

How is this possible?

How can a tree with an abundant, majestic trunk and branches have such a shallow root system?

It's easy. What the Redwoods lack in depth, they make up for in width.

Let me explain. The roots of Redwoods extend one hundred feet laterally, in all directions, and they entangle themselves with the roots of other trees nearby. The Redwoods live in thick groves, where their roots can intertwine and fuse together. This growth technique gives them tremendous strength and stability to withstand strong ocean winds and raging floods.

VALUABLE LESSONS

We can learn valuable lessons from these trees on how to remain standing and even grow, during the storms of life. When we choose life by connecting with other Christians, it's like grafting, infusing and intertwining our roots into theirs. We are not designed to navigate through life alone (Gen. 2:18). Having another brother or sister in Christ can mean the difference between life and death in some instances.

Take Jesus, for example, when He raised Lazarus from the dead. He was close friends with Mary and Martha. When He saw their pain, He was moved with compassion and resurrected their brother. Another reminder is Jesus' final prayer that we become one with each other (John 17:11). He knows breakthrough is found in righteous agreement! So it is a choose-life choice to press into Jesus, together. It releases His power and wisdom.

Jesus's dream for our lives is that we become one with God's other sons and daughters. As we graft our roots into theirs, it shows the world what unity and working together looks like. Infusing our lives with other Christians strengthens and sharpens us, just as "iron is used to sharpen iron" in Proverbs 27:17.

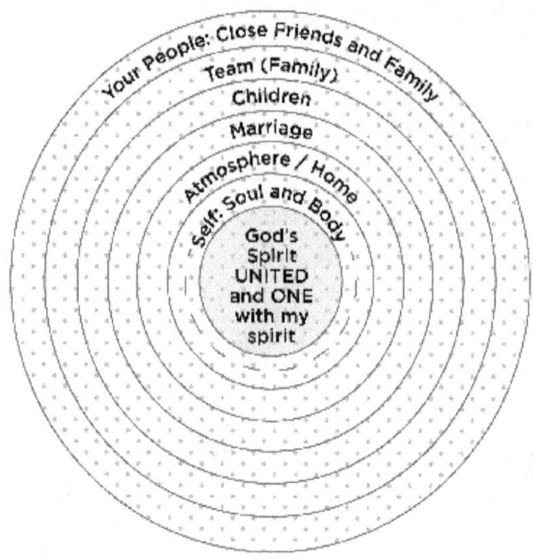

[Figure L—God's Spirit saturating the People ring]

WHEN THE STRUGGLE IS REAL

Growing up I struggled to find my people. Unfortunately, I believed the words spoken over me that I "was a mistake" and I "wasn't wanted." For years I felt like I was different and didn't fit. Outside of my family, I spent most of my time playing soccer. God gifted me athletically and I excelled effortlessly. So as a high-school freshman, I started on the men's varsity soccer team. (And I was only thirteen as a freshman.) Since I played during the majority of each varsity game, I wasn't qualified to play on the junior varsity team with my male freshman and sophomore classmates.

Although it was a blast competing and racing against seventeen and eighteen-year-old males, I didn't feel like I belonged or fit in. Through my high school years, I became recognized by other teams and was awarded All-District year after year and All-State during my senior year. Yet for some reason, this recognition further alienated my connection with others.

Outside of the men's varsity team, I played competitive soccer for other big city teams. All of them were about a two-hour drive away. I played with girls that were my age, but again, I didn't feel like I fit in. Since we didn't go to school together, it was difficult to connect with them regarding their personal lives. They spoke of people, teachers and classmates that I didn't know. Even the dynamic of what had occurred over the past weekend at their school, or in their city was a disconnection for me. When we traveled together, engaging in conversations and other activities was difficult.

THE PEOPLE TRANSITION

In college, when I began walking with Jesus, and was enjoying falling in love with Him, I ceased finding affirmation in some of those closest to me. But that didn't stop the many negative comments unleashed about the movies and songs I no longer wanted to listen to, or watch. I had to let go of the old dynamics with certain people and it was hard. I felt alone as I was growing and changing. I felt like I didn't have permission to share the burning passion inside me.

I tried to find my place amongst my new brothers and sisters in Christ, but when I shared about myself, so they could get to know me, (my broken upbringing, my parents' six marriages, etc....) it seemed to be "too much" for them. They struggled with accepting my story and me, while I was navigating how to find healing and wholeness, in my soul and body. Looking back, it seems this group of Christians was not mature enough to walk alongside me, so God had to place me around a different group of believers. This too was challenging. You may find yourself in the same place, especially, if you have had a rough upbringing. But don't despair, simply ask God at every juncture of growth to show you who needs to be in your life.

MATURE BELIEVERS

Soon after the disconnection with the first group of Christians, I finally felt like I found my people, but I was a lot younger than them. Most of the women had children or grandchildren and sometimes, I felt more like a daughter than a *sister*. Even though they encouraged me to put my "light high on a lamp stand for all to see," and their relationships bred life and freedom—sometimes, I still felt out of place.

However, I was glad we did connect with speaking the same spiritual language. I was grateful we had a common bond of loving Jesus deeply, while we shared story after story about His wonderful and intimate nature. I loved our time spent focusing on Him. And they did too; we had a strong bond together.

In hindsight, I can see God led me in exactly the right direction. It may have been uncomfortable at the time, but I stayed the course. Eventually, I found myself aligning with key connections, those with a high-level purpose, focused on more than just existing in a mundane life.

KEY CONNECTIONS

Connecting with your people for a high-level purpose is more than a gift. It is an absolute necessity to fulfilling your Heaven-story. This concept is like shooting a bow and arrow. The further you draw the bow, (aligning and connecting to your people), the further the arrow, (you) can go. It is rare to find faithful people living the abundant zoë life but when you do, they are a precious present from Heaven. These people truly champion you because they see you through God's eyes.

In the Bible, there are many examples of what happened to people when they encountered their divine, key connections. Not only did this adjoining cause God's Spirit to advance in their life, but also, it connected them to their personal destiny-story. And this released God's grace, favor, and Heavenly assignment to come to fruition—for both the individual, and those in need of rescue and redemption.

BIBLICAL INSTANCES

Just take a look at the chain of events we see in Samuel's life. What a great example of how to connect with your people, so you can connect to your destiny! His mother, Hannah, set the course in motion when she chose to pray for a son. Since she was barren, she needed a blessing from the priest, Eli, in order to give birth. After Samuel was born, he needed to join with Eli, in order to connect with his destiny-story of becoming a prophet. Once Samuel was grown, God used him to anoint David, aligning him with his destiny-story of becoming king of Israel.

Now, for Moses, it was non-negotiable for him to leave his own home, which was Pharaoh's house. He had to find his people, the Israelites, so he could walk into his destiny-story and rescue the nation. Elisha needed to connect with Elijah, so he could fulfill the mandate upon his life. Deborah needed to join with Barak before she stepped into her destiny, bringing forth victory and freedom for God's people. Paul aligned himself to Barnabas (even after Jesus commissioned Paul on the road to Damascus) so that he would step into his destiny-story. Timothy connected to Paul, and *then*, Timothy stepped into his destiny-story. And even Jesus, our God in flesh, chose His people, His twelve disciples, before He began His destiny-story.

It is important to find your people and begin doing life with them. You must intertwine your roots with theirs. Grafting and fusing to others is God's dream for your life. It isn't good to do life alone, especially in seasons when you are learning to overcome and persevere through the vicious storms of life. Besides, your destiny-story may depend on it.

Now is the time . . .

The Expansion of Your Tree: Growing Rings

During all the other transitions that happened in my college years, I remember telling God' "I want to be someone You can trust." I imagined being dropped out of a helicopter at any place in the world, and then in twenty-four months, creating a company of people, focused on loving and worshiping Him. It was my version of, "Here am I. Send me."

Although I didn't realize it at the time, my idea was based on Acts 2:46–47, "With one accord, they continued to meet daily and to break bread from house to house, sharing their meals with gladness and sincerity of heart, praising God and enjoying the favor of all the people. And the Lord added to their number daily those who were being saved."

My desire to impact the world around me was—and is—God's dream for His people. God's dream is for us to expand His love through His Spirit in every ring of life. In Acts 1,

God commissioned His disciples to go into their world and take territory. He instructed them to first invest themselves in Jerusalem (where they currently lived). Then, He instructed them to go to Judea and Samaria (their local community). Finally, He tells them to go to the ends of the earth (the world).

"But you will receive power
when the Holy Spirit comes on you;
and you will be my witnesses in Jerusalem,
and in all Judea and Samaria,
and to the Ends of the Earth."
Acts 1:8

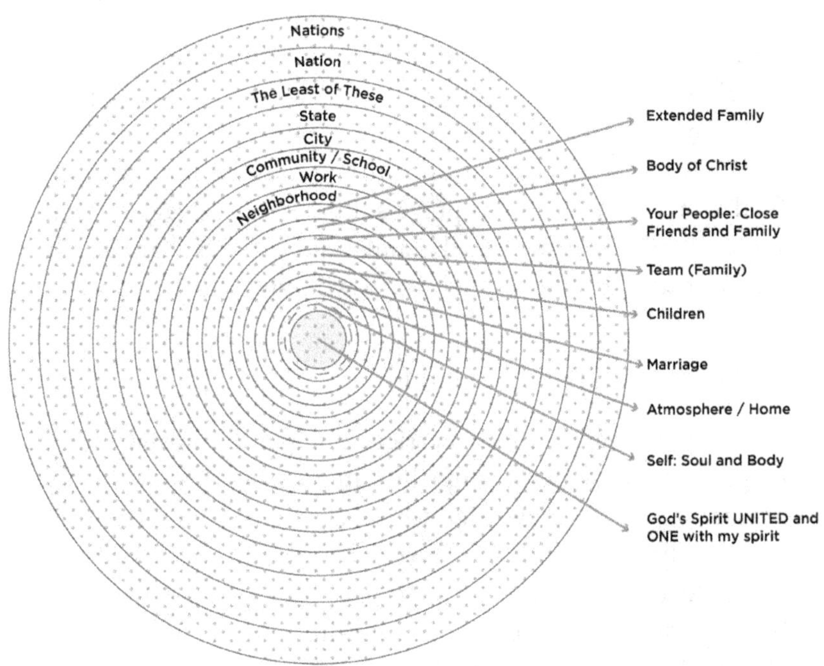

[Figure M—God's Spirit saturating additional rings]

YOUR JERUSALEM

Within your Jerusalem are various mini-sections. Next, we will focus on explaining these areas for hundredfold fruitfulness in our lives.

YOUR EXTENDED FAMILY:

In Acts 16:25–40, a jailer believes in the Lord Jesus and is baptized, and after his decision to receive Jesus, his entire family also gets saved. When I first read this story in college, I loved it. I wanted this for my personal life. I wanted my family to see the decisions I made toward freedom and also say, "Yes!" to Jesus. I desired for them to connect with His abundant, zoë life, by knowing and serving Him only. Like Joshua, my heart, mind and mouth would often proclaim, "as for me and my house, we will serve the Lord."

This should be the cry of all our hearts; we should pray for it and expect it. Although, it may take a while for some, and others may not repent until they are on their deathbeds, God is faithful to hear our prayers. I have seen salvation reach some members of my family, and I am ever so thankful. It may not have reached all *yet*, but I will continue to stand.

YOUR NEIGHBORHOOD:

Years ago, after I was married, our family moved into a neighborhood of almost three hundred homes. I immediately began praying for new friendships with neighbors. I prayed our family would bring a spiritual upgrade while we lived there. After a few months, God gave us a creative idea! We began hosting neighborhood gatherings on a monthly basis. We would arrange food trucks with live music, or rent a projector with a movie screen, complete with a popcorn maker and cotton candy for an outdoor movie night. This was a great way for the neighbors to meet each other, and the kids loved it.

After a few large events, we began inviting families to our home twice a month for a potluck dinner. We spent time discussing Jesus and answering questions about the Bible. Over time, the families began to bond. We started making an impact together through mission trips, and by serving at the neighborhood clean-up day, and by purchasing a water well for an orphanage in Uganda, East Africa.

Loving your neighborhood can be done in a variety of ways. One of my favorite stories is of my dear friend, Adairia. She lives in an area where most are low-income families. One Sunday, after her car had broken down, she chose to take the city bus to church. As she was walking to the bus stop, she noticed dozens of children sitting on the front porches of vacant, abandoned homes. Adairia's heart was burdened. From her core, she could feel God's Spirit washing over her thoughts, emotions and body, until she heard Him speak to her spirit, "they are like sheep without a Shepherd" (Matt. 9:36). Immediately, she was moved with compassion.

She shared her experience with several friends, and we began praying together, asking God for guidance. Within two weeks, she decided to offer them Jesus' love and attention, by hosting, "Jesus' Children's Church." Since that time, Adairia meets with about fifty children, several times a month, in various front yards in her neighborhood. She meets underneath the shade of the trees to discuss Jesus' love and the Bible.

Over the years she's taught them about the power of loving and giving to others. She supplies arts and crafts material, so they can make gifts for their family members. They do this for Christmas, Easter, Mother's Day, and Father's Day. On other occasions, the children take cookies and gifts to the neighborhood nursing home and children's shelter. Adairia creates moments for them to serve "the least of these" in their world, even though, they themselves, experience brokenness, lack and poverty. These children will grow up differently, and affect their world differently, because of the power of the Gospel of Christ.

If your home isn't in a neighborhood, you can still connect with those who live near you. In campus dorms with my soccer teammates, I simply began praying for them. Within a few months, they started coming to me for advice or counsel. It was a natural expansion of my tree to offer the girls shade—a safe place to confide and relax, receive healing and wisdom through prayer.

YOUR WORK:

There are many ways to advance God's love in the marketplace ring. One of my dear family members, Shakira, is a public-school teacher. She consistently prays over the children. Her desire is "for every student to know they are valued, loved, and in a safe space to make mistakes and grow." God's Spirit truly overflows from her, as she sets an atmosphere of Heaven in her classroom. She is aware that many of the children have experienced abuse and considers it a privilege to take territory in this ring of her life. Shakira is one of those teachers that students will remember because of the love (or God's Spirit) she showered upon them.

YOUR JUDEA AND SAMARIA YOUR COMMUNITY/SCHOOL:

One of my best friends has three boys who are high-school athletes. Sally's family is very active in their school and local community. Years ago, she decided to invite other moms to her home for Friday coffee, regardless of how well she knew them. The overall theme of the group was to lock arms and encourage each other to take the next step in their story, focusing on God and His Word.

I've been a part of this group for over five years, and we are tighter than ever. We have shed many tears together, weeping over severe losses and celebrating major victories. What a blessing my friend Sally is to many because of her simple choose-life choice. Her decision to say "Yes!" to Jesus by embracing, loving and gathering moms in the community, has helped them to experience God in a deeper, more personal way.

YOUR CITY AND STATE:

A powerful first step to taking territory in your city and state is by connecting with God's promise in 2 Chronicles 7:14. God always shows Himself faithful, when a person makes the choose-life choice of "humbling themselves, praying, seeking His face and turning from their wicked ways." He promises to forgive the people, and then heal the land that was decimated because of their sin.

One of our couple-friends, the Hills, decided to launch a prayer initiative based on this verse. They invested their own time and money to start a movement in every county across the state. *TheTurnaround.Us* invites everyone to lean into God's redemptive promise by setting their phone alarm to 7:14 a.m. and 7:14 p.m., as a daily reminder to pray. Their goal is to have simultaneous prayer across the state. *There is power in numbers and agreement!*

TO THE ENDS OF THE EARTH THE LEAST OF THESE:

In Matthew 25:40–45, God speaks of the "least of these" who are often overlooked and ignored. It is important for us to structure our lives in such a way, that we can connect with them, and increase God's Spirit in this territory. By deliberately seeking them out, we will have opportunities to share God's love, and speak life and truth to their hearts and minds.

By connecting with the "least of these" we send the message that God sees and loves them. Many of unseen souls are gifts waiting to be unwrapped!

One of my best friends, Annie, lives in a small town where there are over 300 foster children. She kept hearing about the "trash bag kids," foster children who are shuffled from house to house, usually with nothing but a trash bag containing their few belongings, during the foster process. The label "trash bag kids" broke her heart. So she started providing each child with their own sack full of necessities. It was one week's worth of clothes, essential toiletries, a Bible, a notebook, new underwear, socks, and a few special accessories. Her small decision to bless these children is a simple, concrete way of *fostering hope*, as it shows them God's love. The program, *Fostering Hope,* is so impactful that surrounding communities are now using Annie's ideas and resources to bless the foster kids in their areas. Jesus says, "whatever you did for the least of these, you did for me."

YOUR NATION AND OTHER NATIONS

In Psalm 2:8, God beckons, "ask Me, and I will make the nations your inheritance, the ends of the earth your possession." As His sons and daughters, it's our responsibility to release His Spirit to the nations. He wants us to step into our inheritance, as Heaven's ambassadors, and bring God's words and voice to all of creation (2 Cor. 5:20).

What a privilege to live in an era, where every day, hundreds of flights travel across the world. Advances in technology, and global social media platforms, allow us to reach the ends of the earth without even leaving our homes. When God's Spirit is activated in you, by your many, mini choose-life choices, He will naturally overflow from within your core into all your outer rings. You will find yourself thinking and dreaming creatively of how to bless and impact your nation, and the nations of the world. As you press into this, ask Jesus to give blueprints and strategy to mobilize people and gather resources. Set your sights high, and don't dream small! His Spirit will give you the power and confidence to be a bold witness, so you can take more territory. It all begins by increasing His love in your core.

"You will know them by their love."
John 13:35

Now is the time . . .

Water Your Roots: From Roots to Fruits

MY SECRET PLACE STORY

After I had said, "Yes!" to Jesus as Savior at the campus ministry Christmas break conference, I was given a small booklet on "How to Have a Quiet Time." It was so helpful because I had never looked up scriptures. I felt intimidated, navigating through the pages of the Bible. I didn't know the difference between the Old Testament and the New Testament. And I didn't know "the Gospels" referred to the books: Matthew, Mark, Luke, and John, or why they called them "the Gospels." I was truly a baby Christian.

The booklet was a thirty-one day journey that guided me through a variety of Bible passages. It taught me to journal my understanding of what I was reading, and to respond with a written prayer, summarizing what I had learned. Each day, the process took less than half an hour and I loved every minute of it! I wrote with my best penmanship, and I kept my spiral-bound notebook in wonderful condition.

I highly valued this moment of my day, but it wasn't enough. My quiet time always ended with me wanting *more.* I can recall many nights in which it was difficult for me to fall asleep, as this passion burned inside me. I remember pulling the covers over my head and using a flashlight to read my Bible so I wouldn't disturb my college roommate. Then finally, in the early morning hours, I would close the pages and go to sleep. I was learning about Him and how to grow in fellowship with Him, and even feel His Spirit inside me.

It was during these formative years that I began to experience His Presence not only internally, but also externally. One of the most vivid occurrences happened in my car when I was getting ready to play a new song. I reached for a cassette to put in the player, as I had done many times before. But this time was *unforgettable*; I knew I wasn't alone. I recognized His distinct Presence and I was surprised by how easily I could sense Him in the car. I wanted Him to feel loved and respected. So audibly, I said to Jesus, "I've already played the song I want to hear. What song would you like to listen to?"

When I spoke this way, acknowledging Him as a real Person, who speaks directly to my heart, something shifted. And because God is not limited to audible words, His Presence swelled inside my little vehicle. And then the atmosphere grew *thicker*. I was in awe of what was happening. At this moment, I learned how alive and tangible He could be, if I simply acknowledged His Presence. So I began to do it more. I acknowledged Him all the time, and everywhere I went. I understood I was never alone because He was always with me, and He loved it!

Great intimacy progressed, as I included Him in *everything*! I intentionally asked for His feedback on the outfit I was choosing for the day. I acknowledged His Presence, by asking for *two* lollipops when in the bank drive-thru. I even asked the waitress for *two* waters on my weekly, (public) date nights with Him. And sometimes, I would hold the door open a few moments longer, so His Presence would have enough time to walk through. This was childlike faith in action. A tangible way to practice an intangible belief. These public, playful moments with Him in my early years of getting to know Him seemed to catapult our relationship to the next level. But it was my time alone with Jesus lingering in the unseen, secret place that changed me *forever*.

ROOTS

It was here, in the unseen, secret place, that I fell deeply in love with His Word, and where I chose to be still and loved by Him. I didn't know it at the time, but I was watering my roots. This is when I stopped learning *about* Jesus and began meeting *with* Him, as a Person. Jesus was no longer *just* my Savior, but He was my Good Shepherd—the Leader and Guide of my life. By making Him my King, the Lord of my choices, He became more than my Best Friend, He became my Bridegroom, my Portion. He invited me to know Him beyond surface level.

This all happened in the unseen, secret place. It happened each time I chose to water my roots.

"But whenever you pray,
go into your innermost chamber and be alone with
Father God,
praying to Him ***in secret****."*
Matt. 6:6

DEEPER ROOTS

When He became *my Jesus*. And I became *His delight* and *His beloved,* I realized, I was no longer having "quiet times" with Him. And I was not "learning how to become a mature Christian, or follower of Christ." Instead, I was entering into a rendezvous with the Lover of my Soul. I began to understand what it meant for Him to care about the minuscule parts of my heart. I began telling people that I was falling head-over-heels in love with Him. I found myself eagerly pursuing any moment of my day, to be romanced by Him, and to receive His adoration in my core. I honored "coming away with Him" where He revealed many secrets and mysteries of His nature.

All these things thrust me further into the revelation of His love, and as a result, the height of "my tree" grew taller and taller. As I pressed my roots *deeper* through the expansive soil of His Presence, the leaves of my tree appeared vibrantly green and dazzling. My health and fruitfulness began to shine brilliantly, indicating the amount of time I was watering my roots by spending time with Him in the unseen, secret place.

HUNDREDFOLD ZOË ABUNDANCE

What Christians reveal outwardly is merely a reflection of their time spent in the secret place with God. We must invest the rest of our lives expanding and watering the roots of our tree. This nurturing of our roots will assure we bear hundredfold, zoë abundant fruit. And our lives will become like an oak tree of righteousness, radiating God's glory, goodness, and splendor. We will shine far more abundantly than we could ever think, ask, or imagine, through every ring of our lives.

"I pray that you, being rooted and established in love,
may have power, together with all the Lord's holy people,
to grasp how wide and long and high and deep
is the love of Christ, and to know this love
that surpasses knowledge—that you may be filled
to the measure of all the fullness of God."
Eph. 3:17–19

MY REFLECTION

As I reflect on my story, I now see the various stages of my relationship with God. It brings me back to that day on my cozy blanket beneath the expansive oak tree. As I was meditating on His offer of the abundant zoë life, I had no idea where my consistent "Yes" would take me. I had no idea He would give me an eternal treasure in The Zoë Life diagram. I did not know that many others would receive the call to plant *their* roots deep into Jesus and continue to water them.

Now, when I take a deep breath, I enjoy the fragrance of Heaven. I feel the atmosphere of delight, joy and wholeness. My eyes have grown sharp, and my ears, ever so tuned.

I perceive that I am lying beneath a tree of a different kind—a fruitful tree planted by the Lord, nourished by my spirit, unshaken in storms or washed away by floods, a tree that has learned to love.

It is a tree that has forsaken all, for the pearl of great price. It has chosen to connect to its destiny-story people, to bring healing to the nations. It is a tree that expands its branches for her children to learn and grow. It is one where the glory of God shines for all to see. I now live the abundant, zoë full life I have always wanted.

OAK TREES OF RIGHTEOUSNESS

Every part of a tree that we can see above ground first started with its hidden root system. Oak trees of righteousness reveal their beauty and abundance above the surface once they first develop a grounded root system to anchor and support growth. The above-ground expression of trees will reflect what is happening underground. The same is true for us.

If we simply focus on watering our roots, we tap into experiencing the hundredfold, zoë fruitfulness that Jesus supplies.

We will not need to worry and wonder about how to make it happen. Our only focus needs to be one thing … Jesus.

Now is the time . . .

to choose Life!

"How narrow is the gate
and difficult the way that leads to life . . .

. . .and those who find it are few."

Matt. 7:14
Tree of Life Version

Epilogue

It is in the unseen, Secret Place that . . .

. . . you become His Beloved, the One that He loves deeply.

. . . you begin to feel your spirit man commune with God's Spirit.

. . . you experience being undone by Him.

. . . you learn how to fully receive His love emptying into your Self.

. . . you learn how to trust God and taste His goodness.

. . . you are brought by Him to a place where He can trust you.

. . . you overcome old habits, routines, addictions and lusts toward this world.

. . . you grow up, change and mature, learning how to take responsibility and govern your Self with health, purity, and integrity.

. . . you discover who you really are, so that you can learn how you are supposed to live, both within yourself and towards other people.

. . . you learn about God's true character, and it is this revelation of Him that reveals your character—your true Self.

. . . you will become intimidating to the enemy.

. . . your next steps are revealed.

. . . you connect to God's original dream and purpose for your life.

. . . your life resets with order, everything seems to fall in its proper place.

. . . you begin to take territory and the unknown becomes known.

. . . your vision expands.

. . . He satisfies you.

. . . you radiate God's reflection, looking more like Jesus; becoming a visual example of Him in the Earth.

. . . you experience true Life and Freedom.

. . . you discover the majesty of God.

. . . ***you water your roots.***

"Blessed is the person who trusts in
Adonai,
whose confidence is in Adonai.
He will be *like a tree*
planted by the waters,
spreading out its roots by a stream.
It has no fear when heat comes,
but its leaves will be green.
It does not worry in a year of drought,
nor depart from yielding fruit."

Jer. 17:7–8
Tree Of Life Version

About the Author

Kristen is an author, health coach, speaker, creator, and encourager. She wholeheartedly believes in the God-designed zoë life that Jesus came to bring, and it is her passion to help you connect to His abundance too.

"I came that they may have life and have it abundantly."
John 10:10

Kristen carries a call to see the church become healthy and whole in their bodies, souls, and spirits. She has created a number of resources to empower others to make choose-life choices in areas of fitness, food, self, family, and the home. Her heart is to help you navigate life's challenges and bear good fruit in every season. Kristen believes "movement is a medicine for creating change in a person's physical, emotional, mental, and spiritual states." Through her encouragement and guidance, many people are becoming unstuck, making choose-life choices and moving forward in their journey.

Although originally from Tulsa, OK, Kristen currently lives in Redding, CA, with her wonderful husband and three beautiful daughters.

If you're feeling stuck, and ready to take the next step, Invite Kristen to be part of your journey!

www.KristenMarie.com

Connect: hello@kristenmarie.com

DO YOU EAT OUT OF STRESS OR BOREDOM?

ARE YOU AN EMOTIONAL EATER?

DO YOU CONSTANTLY COMPARE YOURSELF TO OTHERS?

ARE YOU TIRED OF THE YO-YO DIET TRAIN?

If you answered "yes," I would be honored to journey with you through *Choose Life Eating*!

In this forty-day program, there are no meal plans telling you what to eat, points to count or special charts to follow. This is not a new diet or a fad. That is why it works! We are going to shift the focus from the food to ourselves. We are going to be the ones who change—from the inside out.

In *Choose Life Eating*, I will teach you how to make choose-life choices when you eat, find freedom from the grip of food and take territory so that you can move forward in your life.

As you apply what you learn, you will discover a new you!

Start your journey:
www.KristenMarie.com

Experience The Zoë Life Master Class

**Imagine author Kristen Marie,
or another Zoë-Life Health Coach, leading you
through a transformational process
where you also connect to the abundant zoë-full life.**

**Find out more at:
www.KristenMarie.com**

Choose Life PEOPLE

Choose Life People is a tribe of Choose Lifers committed to doing life together. We navigate each day through a choose-life lens and look for opportunities to connect to the abundant life God offers us.

We believe God's words in Deuteronomy 30:19 and understand that our choices matter for our lives and the generations that follow.

***Together*, we take steps towards zoë abundant life and freedom!**

"Today I call the Heavens and the Earth
as witnesses against you
that I have set before you life and death,
blessings and curses.
Now choose life,
so that you and your children may live."
Deuteronomy 30:19

Find out more at:
www.KristenMarie.com

CPSIA information can be obtained
at www.ICGtesting.com
Printed in the USA
BVHW062101300620
582537BV00006B/555

9 781640 859548